PUFFIN BOOKS
IN SEARCH OF THE PROPHET

Shahrukh Husain began writing while still at school. Her books include
*Urdu Literature, Demons Gods and Holy Men from Indian Myths and
Legends* and *The Virago Book of Witches*. Her books for children include
Focus on India as well as several books on Islam. She is currently
completing a series for children called Ancient Civilizations. Shahrukh
has also written several screenplays, of which Merchant Ivory's *In
Custody*, adapted in collaboration with Anita Desai, won the President
of India's Gold Medal. Shahrukh lives in London.

Samira Shackle has been passionate about writing since she could hold
a pen. She completed the manuscript of this book just before her
seventeenth birthday. Now eighteen, she is soon to start studying for
a degree in English Literature at Oxford University.

In Search of the Prophet

SHAHRUKH HUSAIN

AND

SAMIRA SHACKLE

PUFFIN BOOKS

An imprint of Penguin Random House

PUFFIN BOOKS

USA | Canada | UK | Ireland | Australia
New Zealand | India | South Africa | China | Singapore

Puffin Books is part of the Penguin Random House group of companies
whose addresses can be found at global.penguinrandomhouse.com

Published by Penguin Random House India Pvt. Ltd
4th Floor, Capital Tower 1, MG Road,
Gurugram 122 002, Haryana, India

Penguin
Random House
India

First published in Puffin by Penguin Books India 2006

10 9 8 7 6 5 4 3

ISBN 9780143335252

For sale in Asia only

Typeset in AGaramond by Eleven Arts, New Delhi
Printed at Repro India Limited

Contents

Searching for the Prophet

S alek shook the hand of the elderly merchant. He was a cunning trader but honest. Salek was pleased at the deal they had struck over their merchandise, all the more because he was sure the old man was dealing with him as an equal, as a fellow in trade and not out of respect to his grandfather's memory.

'Makka will soon be busy again,' said the old man. 'I hear that Muhammad the Prophet plans an expedition.'

Salek was suddenly alert, tense. 'An expedition?'

He clearly remembered the last time the Prophet had travelled to Makka. It was no more than two years ago. The last time he had been in Taif. The last time he had seen his father.

He nodded curtly to the old man and stepped out into the humid night air. The contented feeling of a few moments ago had evaporated and was replaced by that familiar feeling of anger as the memory of that last visit home came crashing back into his mind.

Salek and his grandfather had spent several months in Taif and, as usual, Salek had longed for Sa'd's attention. He had hung around his father, trying to please him in so many ways, to earn the reward of a few moments' attention, an afternoon's play, an evening's conversation. And when that failed, he tried to annoy his father into a reaction. But Sa'd—they called him Al-Shair, the Poet—had been engrossed in his new verse epic. He had barely found time to waste a glance or a smile on his twelve-year-old son. The Poet—it was right that people had all but forgotten his name in favour of the nickname. For that was all that Sa'd was now—not a father, not even a son, but simply a poet.

A feeling of unease settled over Salek in between the waves of anger and grief. His father's epic had been about Muhammad's return to Makka after being forced to leave many years earlier.

'Read it,' he kept telling Salek. 'I wrote it for you.' It was the only thing he ever said to him, over and over again, pointing to the growing pile of parchment. 'My poems. My accounts of Muhammad, Messenger of Islam. Read them. They're for you. And when you have read them, there is something I'll ask you to do for me.'

And that was the message that Salek found when he returned from his next trip. 'Read my poems, Salek. They are my legacy to you.' And that was it. His father was gone.

Salek had searched frenetically for the other half, the unspoken half of the message. What was it his father wanted him to do after he read the poems? He asked all his father's friends, he scrabbled among his writings, but he found nothing.

The verses sat on the table in a corner, gathering dust. He had tried repeatedly to read through them as his father asked. But every time he sat down to read, he felt empty and angry and he could not find the heart or the will.

He walked directly to the heavy, dusty pile now and bent over it slowly, reluctantly beginning to leaf through again. Now was as good a time as any to start reading Al-Shair's work. He would find that last poem—the capture of Makka.

When he found it, Salek moved the flame of the lamp so that it shone more clearly on the script. He bowed over the pages, skimming the lines. It was a long poem and the words brought to mind Al-Shair declaiming with his dramatic gestures, as he described the movements of the Prophet riding with his companions towards the gates of Makka.

Pain shot through Salek. He missed his father even more, now that Grandfather was gone. How different the two men had been. Grandfather had left nothing unanswered but his father had left a void where he should have been, a gaping hollow filled with questions and seething resentments. *Was it me, Father? Was there something wrong with me that made you turn away? Or was it a shortcoming in yourself that took you deeper and deeper into your world of words?*

Yes, Grandfather had left this massive house filled with all kinds of wealth and the entire business in which Al-Shair had never been interested, he had left memories of love and wisdom. Father had left these poems, scrawls and scratches that mocked him. Line upon line, turning into verse upon verse filled with wonderful stories that enticed him into worlds where there was no place for a small boy who soon turned into a sturdy, active and able lad. Tales of wonder, tales of magic, tales of learning, of glorious battles and human suffering and triumph. Less than half the manuscript contained the traditional tales that you would expect to hear from the poets in the marketplace when the caravans had come back.

After the death of his wife Rabia, Sa'd told his father he had no interest in the caravans that provided their living. The last decade of Al-Shair's life had been spent weaving poems that told stories about only one subject. All his work had been about the Prophet.

In fact, so absorbed had he become in the words, the deeds and the achievements of this one man, that he no longer ventured out to tell tales, though he did go frequently to gather what information he could about the Prophet's life. It had come to a point where that had been the sole obsession in his life. Nothing interested him other than researching and writing about Muhammad's doings and sayings. It seemed to Salek that he had lost his father and his mother in a single strike.

'I will take Salek with me,' Grandfather had said. 'He can learn the trade.'

Salek had been five then. He had travelled with his grandfather for nine wonderful years and had seen more of the world than most people dreamt about in a lifetime. And that was why, left alone, at fourteen, he could look around his massive property, study the ledgers filled with his grandfather's exotic script and feel confident that he could preserve and improve his inheritance.

He turned back to the papers on the table in front of him and began reading. It was not yet even three years since this magnificent event. Yet it sounded like a tale hallowed by aeons and embellished by the poet's pen for years.

Salek turned away from the words. Something was preventing him from engaging with these pages. 'Read them,' the note had said. But every part of his mind rebelled. Why should he read these words that had so absorbed his father that his own son had become unimportant to him?

Salek remembered how his father regarded writing about Muhammad as something totally different from his other poetry. Al-Shair had added flourishes and twirls to shape other stories, to accentuate meaning and heighten adventure. But he claimed he had a different rule for the accounts about Muhammad.

'These are history,' he would say. 'It is vital for all of us, every one of us who wants to preserve the truth, to pass it on accurately and in the right spirit.'

He had increasingly got into arguments and debates with other poets and storytellers about this strange, new attitude.

A storyteller, said his fellows, was not a chronicler or a historian—it was his job to build ordinary event into fable, to turn the mundane into the fantastic, to transform poverty into riches. The storyteller, more than anyone else, could deal in the world of potential. And was that not, Al-Shair asked them, what the Prophet Muhammad tried to do? To take humankind beyond the value of gold and status into a world of love and compassion which turned out to be the fabulous highway to a time and space of perfection—a land of milk and honey, which he called heaven. But the others did not approve— or was it just that they could not understand?

'You are turning into a preacher,' they said. 'Find another road to travel. The highways and byways of story are ours. Let us feed from the grain of these fields without contaminating it with your treacherous ideas. Your gruel gives us belly-ache.'

It was one of the reasons Al-Shair had given up his wandering life as a storyteller.

'I applaud anything that keeps him off the streets,' Grandfather had murmured. 'If a man must travel, it should be for serious business, not to squander words. My son doesn't need to tell tales to fill his belly. He has all the wealth and comfort he needs. Better he stays at home if he does not value trade. He could do worse than spend his time meditating on Muhammad. There's no doubt the man has special knowledge and many other good qualities besides.'

So Al-Shair had stayed at home while Salek travelled with Grandfather in preparation for the future when he would be the support of the family. He saw many wonderful places, smelled their smell, felt their feel, and he learned a great deal beside the skills of trading. Once when he told Al-Shair on his return how he had watched the sunset from an oasis and how the sky had changed colours so many times from blue to pink to purple, yellow and red, Al-Shair told him how Muhammad must have seen the same sight when he spent some precious time with his mother at an oasis. He had been seven then.

Salek leafed through the pile again. The story was probably somewhere in these pages. There were so many accounts of this man's doings and achievements—Salek and Grandfather heard them often on their travels. Salek wondered how many Al-Shair had managed to include in his work.

His mind was wandering now. He had a brief memory of some anecdote about Muhammad and a dog on the way to Makka. Had his father left it out? Or had Salek simply failed to take it in as he read the sweeping descriptions of the battle-tale? Certainly he had heard that as the army marched into Makka, Muhammad had seen a mother dog in the path of the oncoming soldiers. She looked distressed, yelping, running about trying to find a way to protect her litter. The story went that Muhammad called the army to a halt and commanded them to alter their route so that they would not cause her distress. But he knew how full of fervour these men were, how keen to get to their goal as soon as possible. And so, he positioned one man by the animal and her puppies to make sure that no breach would take place and that she and her pups would be protected.

When Salek was in Madina once, he had heard the children speak of the Prophet with great love. As they played, they talked about how he had shown them a special trick to fly a kite or hit a ball or even to stay properly afloat while swimming.

Salek returned to the manuscript again. As he leafed through without reading, he found nestled in the sheets a note from Al-Shair. It said he was planning to go to Madina to join the Prophet!

Was his father planning to become a Muslim? The question plagued Salek as he went about his business through that day and the ones that followed. Had his father really meant to abandon him and go to live in Madina?

'What is the power of this Prophet?' he wondered. 'It gets into the minds and hearts of people and makes them willing to give up everything.'

Deep down inside, Salek realized that he was jealous. Jealous of Muhammad, for whom Al-Shair had given up not simply his luxuries, but also in some ways, his son. Earlier—before the last meeting two years earlier—Al-Shair would speak to him when he was home and tell him tales and they would laugh together, but that was small substitute for being a real father. As a poet and a storyteller, he had already defined Salek's fate—the boy had to replace his father and travel with Grandfather. It had become easier after Mother died.

Tears filled Salek's eyes as he remembered his mother's death. Thank god he had been there when she died. He felt he had hardly had any time with her. He thought again of the note he had found among the pages of his father's manuscript.

By the time Salek concluded his business for the day, he had made up his mind. He drew up a list. There were many matters to deal with—nothing complicated, but plenty to do before he could get on with what he had decided. He, at least, was responsible and would discharge his duties. And when he had found a suitable man to leave in charge, he would set out on his journey.

'If Muhammad the Prophet is going to Makka, then I will meet him there.'

The Prophet's Sermon

Salek's eyes were fixed on the figure silhouetted against the sky. Every fibre of his being strained to hear the voice of the man on the mountain. He pushed forward to get closer, trying not to disturb the rest of the huge crowd gathered there.

'Is that the Prophet Muhammad?' he asked as he drew nearer, though he knew before even asking that it was.

'It is Muhammad of the tribe of Quraysh,' an old man replied. 'The Messenger of God and the bringer of peace to Makka.'

Salek nodded, remembering his father's ode.

'The most Arab of us all,' smiled the old man's wife. 'That's what he used to say, anyhow. Because, you know, he belonged to the Quraysh tribe who controlled Makka at that time and Halima of the Bani Sa'd bin Bakr brought him up in the desert.

These tribes and places hold the heart and soul of the Arab people and their tradition.'

There were a hundred questions Salek longed to ask, but he also wanted to listen carefully to what the Prophet was saying. He wanted to find what it was that had enchanted his father. His eyes focused on the tall figure as his words filled the atmosphere.

'. . . *in God's eyes, the most honoured among you is the one who is most God-fearing. An Arab is not superior to a non-Arab . . . nor is a white man superior to a black one or a black one to a white one . . .*'

Salek could not help being enthralled by the voice. He had never before heard this talk of equality. He looked around him at the faces full of concentration and respect.

'*Treat the women kindly, they are your helpers . . .*'

He had great courage, too, uttering thoughts like these in the presence of these tough men, weathered by the desert sun and the hardships of trade and labour.

'*Repay all debts, return all borrowed property, and reciprocate all gifts . . .*'

The powerful voice was beginning to waver. People were straining to hear the words.

'Beware! Only he who commits a crime is responsible for it. A child is not responsible for his father's crime, nor a father for his child's . . .

Nothing of your brother's is lawful for you except what he gives you himself.

Anything that is left in trust with you must be returned to its owner.'

The Prophet leaned towards the man standing beside him. He looked down, humble, and began to repeat every line as the Prophet completed it.

'I am leaving with you the Book of God, if you hold fast to it, you will never go astray.'

Muhammad finished his sentence and waited for his crier to repeat it. The man was gazing at him, deep in concentration. He pulled himself together and spoke. *'Let those who are present convey my words to those who are absent.'*

The Prophet spoke again, addressing the people with a voice full of passion. *'And if people ask you about me, what will you say?'*

The crier squared his shoulders ready to repeat the question. But there was no need. The crowd was responding as one: 'We bear witness that you have conveyed the trust of faith and discharged your ministry and looked to our welfare.'

The Messenger of God pointed towards the sky.

'O Lord, bear witness to it.'

It was odd, how the light seemed to glow around the Prophet's silhouette in the distance. His words gripped and soothed at the same time. As he spoke, streaks of pink smudged the sky behind him, eventually turning to a dark, luminous blue, hung with stars. It was as if time was standing still to allow the people to listen to Muhammad and pray and give thanks. As if it was important to stretch out this moment and make its beauty last as long as possible.

But all things end.

The Prophet said goodbye to the gathered thousands and left.

'Can I find you again tomorrow?' Salek asked the old couple. 'There are many things I want to ask about the Prophet and his life and you seem to know him.'

The old man smiled. 'We knew him when he was a small boy. But then, who didn't know the grandson of Abdul Muttalib around Makka. He was a remarkable little boy. Was he not, Sadea?'

'Honest and truthful as you'll ever find,' added the old woman.

'May I visit you then?' Salek asked.

'Where are you staying tonight?' Sadea asked suddenly.
'Is your family with you?'

Salek shook his head. 'No family. My grandfather brought
me up. He died a few months ago. I'm travelling alone.'

'How old are you?' asked the old man.

'Fourteen last month,' replied Salek. He pointed to the
sack on his shoulder. 'My father left me this legacy. Hundreds
of verses about the life of the Prophet Muhammad. I'm here
to meet him and talk to him and see for myself which stories
are true and which are invented.'

'There are many stories told about him,' the old man
agreed. 'Who knows which are true and which false?'

The old woman placed her hand on Salek's arm. 'I'm Sadea;
my husband is Harith. Stay with us while you are in Makka.
Our house is not far from the Ka'aba. We run part of it as a
guest house so it is full of visitors all year round. You will find
someone there who is willing to take you to Muhammad.'

Salek nodded his gratitude. His years of travelling had
taught him to accept help but remain alert for people who
used kind words and sympathetic faces to hide greedy hearts.
So he made sure to look confident and speak to people as if he

was strong and knowledgeable even when inside he did not feel quite so sure of himself.

He knew better than to let anyone see that just now he felt a little frightened and was wondering why he had taken on this long journey. What was he looking for? He shook his head. All he desperately wanted to understand was why his father had become so obsessed with Muhammad and lost interest in all else.

For now, he was grateful that this old couple had offered him a bed and he was happy to put himself in their charge.

Harith showed Salek to his room.

'Rest a while,' he said. 'Sadea will have something ready to eat. No doubt some of the pilgrims will be coming in search of food—maybe even a bed for a night or two.'

Salek thanked Harith and slumped down on the bed. He would look around tonight for someone who might have access to Muhammad. He wanted now, more than ever, to meet him.

The House of Stories

'Come in,' Sadea beckoned Salek into the hall. 'Sit. You must be hungry. I have many sons. They were always hungry when they were young like you.' She poured out some milk and placed a round of bread and some honey on the table.

Salek thanked her and offered her a pile of dates. 'Something from home,' he said.

Sadea's eyes lit up. 'From Taif?'

Salek nodded. 'I brought them with me.'

'So you are from Taif?'

Salek nodded.

Sadea pressed a glass of milk into his hand. 'Drink. You look as if you need it.'

Salek drank deeply. When he put down the empty glass, he could feel Sadea's gaze on him.

'Tell me,' she said. 'What brings you here?'

'My father was a poet,' Salek explained, not sure how much to say. 'But he stopped writing stories of heroes and battle—in the last ten years, he wrote only about Muhammad. I was curious . . .'

'He would not be the first—thousands give up there way of life to listen to Muhammad's message.'

'But,' said Salek, 'my father did not follow Muhammad or—as far as I know—accept his message. He just kept writing about him. I want to know why.'

Sadea looked reflective. 'My husband and I remember well when Muhammad was born. We wouldn't have been much older than you. It was not an exceptional event. Except of course, we all knew his father had died not long before and his mother kept poor health. We wondered if she would survive the birth. She did, of course. His grandfather Abdul Muttalib came immediately to see him. I recall my parents talking about it—they were worried he wouldn't find a wet nurse.'

Harith had entered the room and had been listening in silence. He spoke now. 'It was the year of the elephant. The twelfth of Rabbi'ul Awwal. A Monday.'

'You remember all that?' Salek was surprised.

Harith laughed. 'It is one of those dates that becomes famous much after the event. But many of us remember the year. It was a hard time.'

Salek's eyes sparkled with interest.

Sadea smiled. 'I met a woman recently, come from the Bani Sa'd lands. She travelled up with Halima that year when the women came to find children. She remembered the events vividly.' She thrust a dish of goat's cheese and olives in front of Salek. 'Eat. I'll try to remember what the Bedouin woman told me.'

Halima's Fortune

It had been a year of famine. The lands where we dwelt, the Bani Sa'd region, were barren to begin with, but the little greenery that did exist slowly turned to brown, shrivelled and crumbled to dust.

Powerless, we watched as the crops dried up and even the flow of sheep's milk began to wane as the animals became weak. We watched and waited and prayed for rain, dreaming of gushing rivulets of water to restore life to our land.

The custom was for women with suckling babies to go to Makka and bring back the infant of a noble family to foster, so that it would be protected from the diseases so common in the big cities. The women hoped to find an extra source of income in payments or gifts from the parents of the child, and were glad to have a connection with a well-to-do family.

In that long, hot, dry year, we set off as usual, but somehow the journey across the desert felt more arduous than usual. The women, the donkeys, the men, all were weak with hunger and lack of water. Still we prayed for rain, dreamt of soft, moist air, and wished that the dry, billowing sands would be saturated with water.

The journey was harder for one woman than for most. Halima was her name. She was a woman from a poor family who had borne the blows of the famine even harder than the rest of us. The she-donkey that she rode was close to collapse with dehydration and malnourishment and walked with a limp. Her infant son, still suckling, rode with her, and the two of them slumped over the donkey's head as they rode, suffering the exhaustion that comes with heat and malnutrition. Her husband, Abi Kabshah, walked alongside, stronger than his wife and son but still dragging his feet along the sand. At times he looked as though he would keel over and leaned heavily on the donkey's reigns for support.

They made a fine picture, the four of them—husband, wife, son and donkey—all of them several feet behind the rest of us and looking as though they had not even the energy to hold up their own heads.

As the journey slowly progressed and nerves were wearing thin, we began to voice our frustration with the family.

'You are holding us back!' shouted one woman.

'Can't you just move faster?' muttered another. 'There will be no children left to nurse at Makka when we get there. *If* we ever get there.'

'If that donkey was moving any slower it would be going backwards!' yelled a third. 'Why don't you just crawl to Makka, it'll be quicker!'

Halima and her family could do nothing. The udders of their sheep began to dry up and they grew weaker because there was not enough milk to quench their thirst. Halima's own milk began to dry up too, until eventually there was not even enough to feed her son. He screamed with hunger all day and all night until his throat was raw and dry and then he fell into an exhausted slumber. Still they dragged on behind the rest of the caravan.

'There will be no infants left by the time we get there,' I heard her sob with fatigue and desperate anxiety for her infant. She was as frustrated as the rest of us with the speed at which they inched along. 'And what mother will give me her child?

It's obvious I don't have enough milk to nurse my own son, let alone someone else's. This whole journey will have been in vain.'

'Don't worry,' her husband comforted her. 'Perhaps God will smile on us and make something wonderful happen.'

'I don't know if we'll make it to Makka,' I heard her tell him. 'We can't hold them back any more.'

After another sleepless night of their infant son screaming and a day of the donkey's limp becoming more pronounced all the time, Halima and Abi Kabshah told us not to wait for them. We went on, a little guilty but relieved that *our* journey, at least, would not be wasted.

We arrived at Makka a fair time ahead of them. The mothers had been waiting for us so all of us soon found infants to nurse.

When Halima finally reached Makka, it was as she had feared. The noble families had already chosen their wet nurses from among the tribeswomen. She wondered what to do. She was disorientated and weak with exhaustion, her throat dry and her stomach empty. And her heart filled with sorrow for the wasted journey she had made her husband and her tiny son endure.

That was when I saw her. I was sitting with my own

daughter on one breast and my new foster-son on the other, smiling dreamily at the two infants.

'Halima!' I laughed, surprised to see her. 'So your lame donkey got you here in the end? Or did you decide to crawl?'

She was too exhausted to laugh at the joke.

In my excitement, I carried on telling her about my new foster-child. 'It was wonderful, Halima. The first woman who approached me was a widow—she would never have been able to give us the endowments I was hoping for. Then I came across another family—very rich, very noble. Look at the boy, can't you see his noble profile already? They brought us into their home, gave us food and water and they have promised us further payment—isn't it wonderful?' I paused, seeing that she was close to tears. 'Halima, what's the matter?'

'I'm very happy for you,' she replied dully. 'But I don't know what I can do. None of the families here need a wet nurse and I can't return home without a foster-child—not after putting my family through that terrible journey.'

I thought hard about what she could do. 'There is one thing,' I said slowly, worried to make this suggestion after what I'd already said. 'That widow I mentioned . . . perhaps she'd be willing to give you her son?'

'I'm sure even she's found a nurse by now,' said Halima miserably.

I shrugged. 'Maybe. All I know is that I saw her approach at least nine of our women. Each one of them refused to foster the orphan—myself included, as you know. No one even looked at her son. Amina. That was her name. She may not be able to give you much payment but an orphan is still better than nothing, I suppose, when you have no other choice.'

I pointed her in the direction of the widow Amina's house, and because she was desperate, Halima went to find her.

She told me later that she knocked at the door. The young slave girl who opened the door said that they had not yet found a wet nurse for the infant, Muhammad. She was sure that his mother Amina would be delighted to see her. She took Halima to the baby and left her with him as she ran to fetch the mistress of the house.

'I was suddenly aware of a sweet smell, something like perfume but—no—more natural than that, something altogether more pleasing,' Halima told us afterwards.

As she inhaled the fragrance, she began to feel peaceful. Energy returned to her sore, exhausted limbs and the tensions of the journey and the famine before it began to dissipate. She walked over to the cot where the baby lay, wrapped in a white woollen blanket. She pulled back the blanket to look at his face.

Her whole being was jolted with the beauty of the child. She was almost afraid to touch him, afraid that she might somehow spoil his perfection.

He opened his eyes and looked directly into hers. Halima was instantly overcome by a feeling of great love for the child who held up his arms to her.

For the first time since the famine, Halima felt she had enough milk in her breasts to feed the child. She lifted him and he drank until he was satisfied.

After that, Halima did not need any time to make her decision. She told her husband right away that they would foster Muhammad. He agreed.

'Do what you feel is right and maybe God will bless us in some way for taking in an orphan.'

During our short stay in Makka, Halima, her husband and their son all quickly returned to full strength and health. From the time that she had seen Muhammad, Halima produced an abundance of milk for both boys. But she confided in us that she was worried about the journey home across the desert on their lame donkey. Would the sickly, limping creature survive another arduous journey? Was it the atmosphere and the wealth of Makka that had revived her family? If so, what would happen once we returned to our barren, famine-stricken homes?

We got ready for our journey back. Halima mounted the donkey, holding her baby son and his new foster-brother, Muhammad. Like everyone else, I was full of doubt whether the beast would move at all, and I dreaded prolonging our journey as it had been on the way to Makka.

Abi Kabshah took the straps and started walking alongside his family. Do you know, that donkey surprised everyone! It did more than hold its own against the other animals—it outwalked them! In the end, Abi Kabshah's family arrived home several hours before the rest of us. It didn't surprise us— Halima's luck had changed dramatically! During the journey, Halima's sheep produced enough milk to feed all four of them, and the whole family was energetic and bright.

'Something amazing has happened,' we whispered among ourselves, as Halima's donkey raced ahead of us and we lost sight of them in the distance. 'Could it be . . .?'

'The orphan?'

'Muhammad?'

'The one we all rejected . . . perhaps it is something to do with him . . .'

'A blessed child?'

'Well, something's certainly changed their luck since they took him on . . .'

As we neared the barren lands of Bani Sa'd, just as dry and brown as when we had left, we saw an amazing sight. The palm trees growing outside Halima's house were now resplendently green and dripped with dates.

Halima and her husband rejoiced—they too were convinced that their foster-child, Muhammad, was in some way blessed.

They became more and more convinced of this as time went by. Their flocks were always plump and full. Some of us would send our sheep to follow them in case they went to more plentiful pastures, but only Halima's sheep returned saturated with milk. Her four children grew healthy and strong, as did Muhammad. And he remained just as beautiful as when she first laid eyes on him, though he quickly outstripped others of his age in growth and strength.

When two years were completed and Muhammad had

been weaned—we began preparations to return our foster-children to their families. But Halima was unwilling. Not only had her foster son brought blessings and good fortune to her family, but they loved him deeply—as much as they did their own children. It was with a heavy heart that they made the journey to Makka to visit Muhammad's mother. This time too, their donkey galloped with ceaseless energy all the way.

Upon arrival they heard that there had been much sickness and several epidemics in Makka of late. Amina was very worried for her young son, and so Halima and her husband readily agreed to undertake his care until further notice. Joyfully, they returned to their desert-dwelling with the blessed child, where they all lived happily for several years.

A few men had entered the room as Sadea told her tale. Now they clapped, bringing Salek to his senses.

'You're a fine storyteller, old mother,' someone said.

'Get on with you,' Sadea grumbled good-naturedly. 'Eat your dinner. The story was for this young man's benefit.'

'And it's a fine account.'

Salek was curious. 'So is there any truth in this business

of Muhammad's presence causing abundance and fruitfulness? I was told he was like any other man.'

'He is a man, but not like any other.'

Salek turned to look at the owner of the strong, cool voice that had spoken. His eyes met the calm gaze of a man no more than twenty.

'If he was like any other man, he would not be a prophet, would he?'

A few men in the company laughed.

'My name is Anas,' said the young man, holding up his hand to silence them. 'Anas ibn Malek.'

'What I meant was,' Salek said, picking his words with care, 'that Muhammad is the Messenger of God but that he is himself a man, not an angel or a superior being. And that means that he does not perform miracles or magic.'

'That is true.'

Salek was puzzled. 'But the woman from the Bani Sa'd said something quite different.'

Anas shook his head. 'Not so. She merely described what happened around Muhammad. No one said Muhammad performed any miracles, or caused the milk to flow from the sheep or the crops to produce a harvest. These were the bounties of God.'

'It could, of course, have been pure chance,' Salek ventured.

'It could indeed,' Anas agreed. 'I do not recall the Prophet ever claiming otherwise. But all acts of Nature are dependent on God's will.'

An old man spoke up now, from a corner of the room. 'There's an event that took place near Halima's house after Muhammad returned. It demonstrates without a doubt that God was preparing him for prophethood.'

Salek felt his memory stir. 'I'm sure that my father told me about it. He described it as the cleansing of the heart. I can't remember his words, nor can I recite as he did. But I recall the story clearly.'

'Tell us then,' said the old man. 'You heard the Prophet tell us to spread his words. And if you have some detail wrong, one of us can correct you.'

An Encounter with Angels

Have we not opened your heart and relieved you of the burden which weighed down your back? (Surah 94)

Muhammad played among the dunes with Halima's sons. The sun was still low and so the sand had not heated up. Suddenly Halima's boys froze, staring at a point behind Muhammad.

'What is it?' he asked, turning to see.

Three creatures of light stood behind him. They were angels—tall, human-like and glowing with a clear light. Muhammad narrowed his eyes, trying to see into the dazzling brightness. One of the creatures was holding a silver jug. The second held a green dish, sculpted from emeralds, containing fluffy, white snow. The third hovered behind them, silent, watchful.

Wordlessly, the first of them reached out, took Muhammad's hand and led him up a small hillock in the distance. The others followed.

Suddenly he stopped, reached across and passed his hand over Muhammad's stomach. It fell open.

'It doesn't hurt at all,' thought Muhammad in amazement.

The creature of light was an angel. He reached into the cavity of Muhammad's stomach and drew out his intestines. Muhammad watched as he took some snow from the emerald tray and washed his intestines before carefully replacing them.

The second angel stepped forward, laying down his tray of snow on a rock beside him. He turned to the first creature and said, 'You have done what God asked. Go now.'

The second angel reached into Muhammad's open body and took out his heart. Once again, Muhammad felt no pain or fear. He watched, fascinated, as the creature split his heart in two and deftly removed a black speck from it.

'That is Satan's part in you, Beloved of God,' said the angel, throwing away the black speck. He took some snow from the emerald dish and washed the heart carefully. When he was satisfied that it was clean, he replaced it in the cavity of Muhammad's chest.

The third creature had been silent so far, but now he stepped forward with a set of large scales, and spoke. 'You may leave now. You have done God's will.'

He knelt beside Muhammad, and gently passed his hand across the opening in his body. Immediately it was sealed. 'Now he must be weighed against ten others.'

He raised his arms and the next moment they were surrounded by a crowd of people.

The third angel placed Muhammad on one side of the scales and ten men on the other. Both sides swooped down. Then, the one bearing Muhammad rose, swayed slowly in mid-air, then sunk well below the other and stayed there. The four-year-old boy was heavier than ten adults!

'He would be heavier even if we weighed him against a hundred people!' said the third angel. 'Let him go.'

As he spoke, the first and second angels reappeared. Gently they led Muhammad down the hill. They kissed him on the head and between his eyebrows.

'You will never be afraid because you are the Beloved of God,' they said. 'And if you knew how much good you will do in the world, it would make you very happy.'

They asked Muhammad to sit down, and when he was settled, they took flight.

Muhammad craned his neck, watching them as they

went higher and higher into the heavens and vanished beyond the skies.

The old man sighed. 'What beauty! What a magnificent image! Angels flying from hot, desert sand into the cool blue of the skies. And that is why people love a poet. He has the power to transform ordinary events into fabulous ones.'

Sadea was in a world of her own. 'That is so. That is so,' she agreed, as if trying to find a way to describe something in her mind beyond those words. 'But perhaps . . . perhaps the event is already fabulous and we ordinary folk just fail to see it. Think, for instance, of when a child is born—we rejoice. It is a wonderful moment. But then it is also a common occurrence.' She looked through the window at the thronging crowd. 'All these people are proof of it. They were all babies once.'

She took a sip of her mint tea and her eyes looked into some faraway world. 'But perhaps the poet can see things that we do not—something wonderful and miraculous that we others miss because our minds are so filled with everyday thoughts. And then, he looks for the language and the images that describe those wonderful, miraculous things.'

'You mean,' said Harith, 'he senses the involvement of the divine?'

Sadea shrugged, getting up to go to the kitchen. 'Perhaps,' she said slowly. Her voice softened to a murmur. 'There was indeed a godly presence there that day when I visited Amina before she left to see her family in Yathrab. I have never felt it before or since. It flowed between her and her son . . . but how can I find words to describe it? I'm not a poet.'

Salek followed Sadea out of the room. 'I have a lot to do,' she said. 'Be off with you. Go and talk to those men.'

'I wondered what you meant when you spoke of that godly feeling.' Salek made himself busy around the kitchen, clearing and cleaning. His question hung in the air but the old woman said nothing for a long while as she covered up the milk and yoghurt and put away the cheese and bread.

'I'm not a poet,' she repeated, 'just an ordinary old woman. But I was not the only one who felt that extraordinary quality about Muhammad when he was a boy. He was just six at the time—and you'd catch him observing you with a look of wisdom or knowing that was unusual for a child of his age. And his smile could light up your entire soul.'

Salek pushed back a feeling of slight impatience. He could see nothing godly in what she described. Unusual, perhaps even a little uncanny, but not much more.

Sadea was looking at him strangely. 'You don't understand, do you?' she murmured. 'And that is why we need poets. All I can say is, if you saw it, you'd recognize it. That slave girl who worked for his mother saw it too. What was her name . . . Baraka. She never stopped talking about the child. And how she pined when Halima took him away. You would have thought she gave birth to him.'

A Mother's Love

L ife in Makka was exciting. The boy witnessed sights and
sounds that he couldn't have imagined in the desert of
the Bani Sa'd.

I could see he missed Halima and her children but he was
thrilled to be back with his mother and the rest of the family.
Muhammad had cousins and uncles and his grandfather Abdul
Muttalib to distract him and keep him busy.

Amina encouraged Muhammad's friendship with his
cousins. She never complained about her illness, but she realized
it would be better for her son if he had a larger family to enfold
him and protect him if she died while he was still young.

It made her sad that her husband had never seen their
son. But it was important that Muhammad would not be
disadvantaged because he had no father. It made her happy

that his grandfather, a powerful man in Makka, adored him as did his many uncles.

I used to watch from a distance as Abdul Muttalib lifted him on to his bed, where none of his sons or grandsons dared to climb. And the great patriarch would walk around the town with Muhammad on his shoulders.

Muhammad was happy in those days. There was no doubt about that. But however happy he was, however much he enjoyed being with his grandfather and cousins, he never forgot about his mother, her health, her well-being. And when he knew she was unwell, he never left her side.

'It's time I took you to Yathrab,' Amina told Muhammad one day. 'You will meet my brother and the rest of my family.'

Muhammad spent the next days in happy preparation for the trip. When at last they arrived in Yathrab, all his hopes were fulfilled. His cousins were delighted to see him and determined to give him a good time. They taught him many new activities, and the child was quick to learn most things. He took to the water like a graceful fish when they gave him his first swimming lessons. Though he was younger than most of them, he kept up with their games. But we all have a sticking point—Muhammad's was the kite. Whether it was just that the wind fell when he tried to get the thing to fly and rose when he handed it over to another one of the children, I can't say. But I watched him over and over again, casting the thing in the air, tugging the string, running along with it. But would it mount the air and fly for him? Never. Not that he was one to fret over failure in games. There was so much else he was good at that it remained a challenge without becoming a sore point.

Then it was time to leave. Amina sent me to find out when the caravan would depart. Muhammad was sad to say goodbye to his Yathrab family. But he was a child who always saw the cheerful side of things. As he said goodbye to his cousins, he was already preparing to be reunited with his kinsfolk in Makka.

During the journey, I thought I sometimes caught a glimpse of the slightest furrow in his brow, the lightest shadow across his face, the tiniest droop to his neck when Amina's voice grew soft or her lids began to flicker. He would bring her water and juicy fruits and create a shade over her head to make her comfortable. Even at six, he was showing the compassion and generosity of soul that eventually won him the love of thousands.

Amina revelled in the love of her son. 'I have been blessed,' she would tell me. At night when the caravan stopped, the fires were lit and the food cooked, she would rest with her son and tell him tales about his father and their life together. I listened too, sitting a short distance away. His favourite was the story of his birth.

Amina painted a happy picture. They enjoyed great respect as members of the tribe of Quraysh and the family of Abdul Muttalib. Muhammad clapped his hands when Amina mentioned her father-in-law.

'Are you taking about my grandfather?' he asked, laughing. 'The same man on whose bed I play beside the Ka'aba?' Amina, and even I, would laugh and remind Muhammad that he was privileged.

'I have seen your uncles chasing their sons away if they went too near Abdul Muttalib. You are his favourite. You are the only one allowed on Abdul Muttalib's bed.' Muhammad would glow with pleasure, but never once then or the years that followed, did I hear him boast or brag about it.

Amina told Muhammad his father Abdullah was often away on family business, leading his father's caravans to Taif and much further afield. But when he was in Makka, he was a loving and kind husband who would have been a wonderful father. But fate took him from them long before his time. She thanked God that he did not die alone and without family in some strange town but surrounded by her family in Yathrab.

All men want a son to carry on their name. Abdullah had been too young to make his own fortune, but they had lived in comfort and he was sure that one day he would provide plenty for his family. Then one day, Amina made him very happy.

'Last night,' she told him, 'I heard the voice of an angel telling me that I would give birth to a son. He told me to name him Muhammad. Later, I noticed a light coming from me, and in its glow, I saw the castles of Syria.' It made her feel happy to know that Abdullah had been able to rejoice with her at the news of his soon-to-be-born son, even if he had not survived to see his birth.

During those days on the journey, I saw Muhammad grow closer to his mother. Yearnings stirred up in me—I had a mother too once, but it was only in my wildest dreams that I imagined being with her again. Watching my mistress wrap her son in the soothing mantle of her love made me remember how a mother's love feels.

But I could also see that Amina was growing weaker. At night when Muhammad was seeping soundly, she would ask anxiously, 'How long before we get to Makka? Do you think, Baraka, that I will see our home again?'

At last we arrived at the oasis of Abwa. The caravan stopped, the travellers ate and rested. When Muhammad was absorbed in a game with the other children, my mistress beckoned me.

'Baraka,' she said, 'fetch the leader of the caravan. I need to speak to him.'

The man arrived and stood respectfully before my mistress.

'I am weak,' Amina said. 'I do not want to hold back the other travellers. It may be necessary for me to stay behind.'

'But, my lady, what will I tell Abdul Muttalib?' the man protested.

'Explain that it was my decision,' Amina replied. 'My son and Baraka will stay with me. I will be looked after. I will recover after a few days of rest, in time to join the next caravan back.'

The man thought carefully. He had a responsibility to the other families as well, and he could see that Amina was worn out by the journey.

The next morning, as dawn broke, the travellers awoke and prepared for the next stage of their journey.

Amina put her arm around Muhammad's shoulders. 'We will stay here for a while. We will resume our journey when the next caravan arrives.'

The days that followed were like a wonderful dream. For

the first time in his life, Muhammad had his mother exclusively to himself. The way he took care of his mother would have won high praise even for an adult. Mother and son gave each other strength and joy.

On some days, the energy seemed to surge from Amina and she would swim in the lake of Abwa with Muhammad. He would walk in the desert. He knew all about deserts—after all, he had been raised among the Bani Sa'd—and could tell one dune from another, and judge the direction of the winds from the way the ripples lay on their surface.

One day when he returned from a walk, Amina was sitting by the water's edge. She was excited like a girl, with her cheeks glowing and her eyes sparkling with fun.

'Come here, son. See what I have for you.' She held up a kite she had made from a fallen palm frond, bound together by the jute fibre from the bark. 'I'll teach you to fly it.'

The next moment, she was running across the shores of the lake, pulling the string. The kite sailed along behind her for a moment. Then it caught a gust of wind and began to soar. Muhammad clapped his hands.

'Here,' Amina handed him the string and guided his fingers round it. I saw him cast a quick glance up at the kite. His face lit up. The kite was still coasting along like a cloud. Muhammad began to run. The kite soared in the air, up, up above him.

If that smile, that moment of triumph and joy was the last picture the mother and son had of each other, then it was in itself a blessing. Amina did not live many hours after that. It was as if God had provided them with this short but intense period of bliss before they had to say goodbye.

I was just a slave girl—thirteen, maybe fourteen—but I swore I would get Muhammad back under his grandfather's protection in Makka, and as long as the gods allowed, I would serve him with my whole being. Anyone who had seen him through that journey to Madina and back would have known that he was a very precious child.

Salek turned away from Sadea as she finished her story. He did not want her to see how his eyes had filled with tears at the memory of his own mother. The weariness of the last few days suddenly weighed down on him.

He turned to Sadea. 'It has been a long day,' he said. 'With your permission, I'd like to retire now.'

Lying in bed, looking at the stars through his tiny window, Salek thought it was strange that like him, Muhammad had lost a much-beloved mother when he was still a child. He thought about the strong sense of pain he must have experienced as a small boy. It had brought back his own pain, the grief that he had never properly expressed because he had thrown himself into the business that his grandfather had offered as an antidote to his loss. He wondered if it was because of his loss that Muhammad was so full of love and compassion for others, particularly children.

Salek's last impression that night was of the vast sky, blackened by night, brightened by starlight.

Usually, when Salek was in a strange city, the demands of commerce kept him busy. There were the basic tasks of unpacking the stock and examining the goods to check they had not been damaged in the journey. Then there were deals to be done, transport arranged and sales made.

But this time Salek had none of those concerns. His mind roamed free, absorbing impressions and exploring questions that he had never before had time to consider. He had a mission, he knew, but it was a search for something he could neither buy nor sell, something he could not see in order to test for quality and content. His quest was for something intangible, something that would lead him to understand what it was his father had seen in this new religion and its leader.

Salek sought out people who knew the Messenger, asked questions and became more and more convinced that he must try and seek a meeting with him. Everyone told him that the Messenger was not a proud or arrogant man and would welcome anyone who went to meet him. Only, when Salek went to the places he could be found, he saw Muhammad thronged by men and women and was forced to leave disappointed.

But one thing he was not short of. The Arabs were a people who loved stories, and Makka was full of men and women willing to sit down in a shady spot and recall an event about Muhammad, the son of their soil, the true Arab, Al-Amin, the Truthful One. Nearly every street around the environs of Ka'aba led to a story connected to the Holy Prophet. There were still people here who had known him as a young man, even as a boy, and as his fame grew, they had passed on their knowledge to the next generation. Perhaps the accounts would clarify something to him of what went on in the mind of his father and lead to a better idea of what he wanted to ask the Prophet when he finally met him.

That night, as he sat at Sadea's table, surrounded by the nightly gathering of men spilling their memories, he asked about Muhammad's childhood.

'His grandfather looked after him for a while,' Harith said. 'When he died, his uncle Abu Talib took care of him. But he had many responsibilities.'

'Oh yes,' laughed an old man. 'Abu Talib was a just man and a good one. But he insisted that everyone in his house earned his living. And Muhammad was no different. He tended the livestock and did any chore that came his way. He was the person working the hardest in that household.'

The old man's eyes wandered and Salek could see them filling with memories.

'Tell us,' he said. 'Tell us what you remember.'

And the old man began his tale.

What Bahira Saw

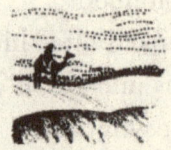

We had been preparing for the trip to Syria for some time—the second great caravan trip of the year. Carefully bound packages of incense, bunches of folded cloth, mounds of leather and boxes spilling over with dates surrounded us. Most people in the town were involved with trade in some way, and the town seemed saturated with craftsmanship and sweet scents. All of these goods were loaded up, packed into caravans and strapped onto camels.

One of the traders, Abu Talib, had recently adopted his orphaned nephew, Muhammad, and planned to leave him at home during the journey. However, the young Muhammad quickly formed a strong attachment to his uncle and the distress was evident on his face every time the journey was mentioned. Eventually, Abu Talib softened and did not have the heart to leave the poor little boy at home.

'I'll allow you to come with us,' he said, 'as long as you make yourself useful. You can learn a trade.' So Muhammad accompanied us as an apprentice camel driver.

We set off, travelling through mountains, deserts and cities. Muhammad was a very quiet boy but his interest quickened as we passed the historical sites. He wanted to know about King David as we passed Rabbath Ammon, and he asked to hear other stories, seeming intrigued by our talk of Biblical characters, history and local mythology.

One of the camps we set up on our journey was in bustling Basra, the capital of Syria. The city had high walls all around it, and a newly built cathedral whose dome was visible from miles away.

As we rode to the campsite, I saw a lone figure on the landscape, his gown billowing around him as he stared at our party with unwavering eyes. It was Bahira, a Christian monk who lived in a hermitage far up in the mountains. I thought nothing of his presence—Christians had inhabited the monk's cell in this place for many years. We had seen him before—and he us—but he had always been quite indifferent to our presence.

At first I assumed he was musing or meditating or thinking holy thoughts, or whatever monks are supposed to do. But then I noticed that his gaze was focused intently on our party and followed us as we moved. He seemed to look past me and the other men, staring instead at the very back of the group where clouds of dust were rising behind us.

I looked behind me to see what was so captivating the monk. At the tail end of the party, Muhammad was trudging along. As the apprentice camel driver, he was very low in the hierarchy of the group—and one of youngest. The huge puffs of dust that rose up around him all but obscured him and yet he seemed to be the focus of the monk's unwavering gaze. I felt slightly uncomfortable—why was Bahira staring in this way?

I learned later that he saw a cloud of light accompany the group. At first, he dismissed it as one of the tricks that the desert plays on your eyes and kept trying to ascertain whether it was really there and who it was following. He was not staring at Muhammad—indeed, he could not even see him due to the dust and the distance—but at the spot just above his head, where this cloud of light floated. However, as this illuminated cloud was not visible to me, or the other members of the party, there was something unnerving about the concentrated gaze.

As we set up our camp, Bahira continued to stare at us.

Then for a while, he disappeared. Later, he returned and called out to us, 'Tribe of the Quraysh! I would be honoured if you would all eat with me tonight.'

This was remarkable—the monk had barely so much as greeted us on past trips! I felt somewhat uneasy at this new attention. But after all, he was a holy man, and so it was very unlikely that his motives could be suspect. My tribesmen gladly accepted his offer of a feast. Rations for the journey are always restricted and the meals simple. It was well known that there were vast stores of food in the hermitage, constantly renewed by donations from pilgrims.

'Bring *all* of your men,' he said. 'A feast will be prepared for all of you. Old and young, free and enslaved, you shall all eat with me. I look forward to seeing you.'

When the time to visit Bahira arrived, in our enthusiasm, we forgot his injunction to bring everyone. After all, someone had to look after the goods and the camels. As the youngest and lowliest in rank, Muhammad was left behind to look after the goods and the camels. I remember looking back at him as we left, laughing and joking. He sat quietly on a tree branch. He did not make a single plea or complaint, but it was clear from his face and his slightly slumped body that he was sad and withdrawn. I felt a pang of guilt, but did not voice my concerns and went back to the jokes of my tribesmen.

Bahira stood smiling when we finally arrived at the opening to his cave dwelling. He greeted us all formally as we entered one by one. But he was staring again, intensely, at each man's face, searching for I don't know what. I could not help squirming under his keen gaze as he scanned my face, and when he finally let go of my hand, relief surged through me. Finally, we all entered the house but Bahira lingered in the doorway, quickly glancing over all of us again, with that same searching look. His expression had changed to one of confusion.

'Are you sure you remembered to bring all members of the party?' he asked.

'Everyone's here,' said someone.

'*Everyone?* You didn't mistakenly leave anyone behind? Anyone at all? A slave?'

The men all looked blankly at each other.

'Well, we didn't bring everyone exactly,' I heard myself say. 'We left Muhammad behind.'

As I spoke, we all began to feel incredibly guilty. The image of the little boy all alone on his branch settled in my mind and would not leave.

'I could go and fetch him,' I offered.

This cheered everyone up, including Bahira, who continued to look very thoughtful.

I ran back to the camp.

'Muhammad!' I called. He was still sitting in the tree where we had left him, huddled against the tree trunk and staring into space. He turned around as he heard my voice. I held him in my arms and hauled him off the tree-branch.

'You'll join us for dinner, after all.'

His face lit up and together we returned to the hermitage.

Bahira was the perfect host, joking and laughing with his guests. Others might have ignored a small boy but Bahira turned to him as we walked in, smiling and greeting Muhammad with as much respect as he had shown us. He gave him that same probing look but this time it was not as intense as it had been with the rest of us. It was as though he did not have to look as hard to find whatever it was he was searching for.

We sat down to dinner.

'Come and sit here,' Bahira said to Muhammad, patting

the seat beside him. Though he still talked to everyone, his attention was focused on the small boy. He asked him a great many questions, about his family, his faith, his daily habits and routine—even his ambitions for the future.

At first Muhammad seemed a little awkward. Since his grandfather's death, no one had paid him so much attention. But he soon began to relax and answer Bahira's questions comfortably and eloquently.

I was struck by the monk's interest. He seemed intrigued by what Muhammad had to say. He looked thoughtful and reflective after some of the boy's answers and occasionally smiled to himself.

As we got up after the meal, Muhammad turned around and stretched his arms up above him as he yawned (let us not forget that he was just a little boy—it was late for him to still be awake!). His shirt rose slightly, exposing a red welt on his back. Bahira stopped dead in his tracks and stared. The colour seemed to drain from him for a moment, before an excited half-smile settled on his lips and he composed himself once more.

When it was time to leave, Bahira took Abu Talib aside. 'I have something important to tell you,' he said. 'May I trouble you to stay a while longer?'

Abu Talib agreed. The rest of us continued to the camp, but Abu Talib later told me what Bahira had said.

'What is your relationship to the boy?' Bahira asked Abu Talib.

'I am the boy's father,' Abu Talib replied.

Bahira looked confused.

'But that's impossible . . .' he said. 'The boy must be fatherless.'

'I am his father by adoption. We took him in after my brother died,' Abu Talib explained, wondering how this monk knew so much. 'He's my nephew.'

'I have observed the signs of prophethood in Muhammad,' Bahira told him, his face bright with joy. 'I began to suspect it when I saw the cloud of light hovering above his head.' When Bahira had seen the illuminated cloud over our caravan, he had remembered St John's prophecy in his Gospel that 'the comforter' would come to earth. He had hurriedly looked up the books for information on the signs of prophethood and how to recognize them. When he looked over at our camp and saw the cloud of light still hovering over the branches of the tree where Muhammad sat, he became more and more convinced that he was right. It was then that he invited us to the feast, being so sure that 'the comforter', the long awaited one, was among our party.

Bahira explained that the boy's conversation had confirmed what he needed to know. The final sign, he said, was the welt on his back—the seal of prophethood.

Bahira told Abu Talib that Muhammad had a great future ahead of him. 'You must take him back to his country,' he warned. 'And keep him safe from those who wish him harm— no one must find out what I know.'

After recovering from his original shock and disbelief at this news, Abu Talib took Bahira's words seriously. For the rest of the journey he made more of an effort to keep Muhammad close by. He remained quiet about what Bahira said but made plans for a swift return to Makka.

Salek listened to the many stories that followed about Muhammad's growing up years. He was a popular figure in Makka, it seemed, always willing to help anyone in need, and with a ready smile. He accompanied Abu Talib on many a caravan after that first one and in time became an able trader. Then one day as he walked down the street, he received an offer that changed his life.

The Caravan to a New Life

Maysara saw a man coming down the road. He was tall; taller than most men. And he looked strong.

'Muhammad. That must be Muhammad,' he thought as the man rapidly came nearer. Maysara stepped quickly out into the road in front of him.

'Excuse me, sir,' he stammered. 'I am Maysara, slave of Khadija, daughter of Khuwaylid bin Asad. I have a message from her.'

Muhammad stopped and smiled at the boy. Immediately Maysara felt a sense of relief. There was a warmth about Muhammad, and great kindness in his face. Not that Maysara expected kindness. Slaves were not treated like other humans. Their owners often talked about them in their presence, as if they couldn't hear or feel, forgetting that some of them had once run free around their homes and had been loved and cherished by their families and communities, just like the people who bought and sold them in the marketplace. But once they had been bought and sold, they were expected to forget their past and simply do as they were told. If they were reasonable lucky, as he was, then they had a great deal to be thankful for.

Khadija, Maysara's mistress, was not only kind, she was also smart in business, fair-minded and generous. Maysara counted himself lucky to be working for her.

'My lady has asked me to tell you that she needs the skills of a man like you and she would like to discuss some business.'

Muhammad started to follow Maysara, but soon the boy was huffing and puffing trying to keep up with his long, swift strides. At last they arrived at Khadija's home.

Khadija was the richest woman in all Makka. Her husband had died, leaving her with a large trading business and she had managed it single-handedly and well. She dealt fairly with the men who worked for her. Her caravans travelled all the major trade routes and she gave a share of her profits to the men who carried her merchandise. That way, she made sure as far as she could, that they remained loyal. The leaders of Makka had great respect for her and if she had wanted to remarry, a hundred men would have rushed forward to offer their hand. But Khadija was an independent woman.

'I am sending an important consignment of merchandise to Syria,' she told Muhammad. 'And I need someone like you, skilled in commerce and travel. People call you Al-Amin, the Truthful One—and that is the quality I most require. In return for that, I will give you a higher share of the profits from the expedition than usual.'

Muhammad accepted Khadija's offer and began preparations for the caravan to Syria. When the expedition was ready to leave, Khadija spoke to him again.

'You remember the boy Maysara, who brought you to me,' she said. 'I would like him to accompany you on your trip.'

Muhammad approved of the idea of a young slave boy being taught a skill. It would give him a chance in life.

Muhammad and Maysara left Makka with plenty of food and water. The expedition followed the sun north and it was not long before they found themselves in the desert, with golden sand stretching out on every side of them. Muhammad explained to Maysara how they would make sure they didn't lose their way; how they could tell where they were from the position of the sun during the day and the formation of the stars during the night; how the rippled surface of the sand was formed and how best to shelter from the wind and sand during a storm. At night, around the fire, the men would roast their meat and sing their songs and tell amazing tales of their adventures. Some of them had experienced wonderful and terrible things—but there was always a solution. There were ways of finding the right path again if the caravan strayed off course, or of curing a camel or a rider who fell sick. But Maysara learned there was one thing for which there was no real solution. For a few hours each day, the sun would rise high in the sky and grow in intensity until its heat felt like a smouldering bar of iron on their skins. And there was no refuge from it, no tree, no hut, no cloud behind which they could seek shade.

When the heat was unbearable, the men stopped and sheltered behind their camels as they watered them. But they would be on their way too soon and the sun would once again sear their skin and burn their heads, seeping through their clothes and head-protection as they rode along. Maysara saw the men wilt and droop. Some of them clung to their camels, resting their bodies along the length of their necks, as if all the energy was drained from them. Then they would let their minds wander away into the darkness of the night, trying to sink in their imagination into its quiet coolness. Or they would focus their minds on the journey's end, reminding themselves and each other of the comfort of the city where there were beds to rest and tables to eat at. In this way, the gap between their starting point and their destination shortened.

'Look!' Maysara shouted one day. 'I see a house.'

He could feel the sense of excitement as the caravan picked up pace and moved quickly towards the house. They had reached habitation. There would be a watering hole near it. And somewhere not too far away, a city.

Soon they stopped their camels and, after they had fed and watered them, they walked towards the house which stood beside a cluster of trees. A few men went in and enquired about food. The house belonged to some monks and they were happy to offer the travellers hospitality.

Maysara came out to find Muhammad who was standing outside, enjoying the shade of a tree. He was looking around him, taking in the city skyline in the distance. Maysara had noticed that Muhammad enjoyed the company of others but seemed to gain great pleasure from a few moments of solitude. He was not a man of many words; he spoke only when he had to. He could be silent for long periods, yet his silences never made people feel uncomfortable. Perhaps because the expression on his face was always open and friendly.

Maysara decided not to interrupt him. Quietly, he returned to the cool darkness of the monks' cell. As his eyes grew accustomed to the dimness, he noticed a monk looking at him curiously.

'Who is the man resting in the shade of the tree?' he asked Maysara.

'That is Muhammad,' Maysara replied. 'Of the Quraysh clan.'

For a few moments, the monk was lost in thought. 'Only prophets have ever rested in the shade of that tree,' he said at last.

Maysara's heart lurched but he said nothing. He knew Khadija would ask him about Muhammad when he returned to Makka but he had never imagined that he would have to report a prediction of prophethood.

Nor did the monk's words prepare him for what he saw one day on the return journey as the caravan passed doggedly through the noonday rays of the sun. As the rows of camels with their leathery skins moved rhythmically forward, the men were slumped against their animals. Muhammad, however, was riding erect. Maysara narrowed his eyes, trying to focus his vision. What were those tall shapes on either side of Muhammad? He could clearly see two pale figures on either side of Muhammad, forming a canopy so that a deep shadow fell over him as he rode along. Maysara rubbed his eyes and looked again. Who were these creatures with their strange, silvery gleam?

'I think,' Khadija said thoughtfully when Maysara narrated this tale on his return, 'that these are the beings my cousin Waraqa mentions. They are called angels.'

But Maysara was still unsure whether he had really seen these beings called angels or whether the sun's glare had played tricks with his sight.

Khadija had been very busy since they returned. The caravan had brought back many valuable goods from Syria, which proved popular in the marketplace. Even Hind, Abu Sufyan's wife, was said to have praised them highly. All this meant that Muhammad lived up to his reputation as an honest man and a skilled merchant.

Khadija listened carefully to the other things people said

about him. He was a kind man who never intentionally hurt any living being. His manners were perfect. In fact, hardly anyone had a bad word to say about him. Muhammad, she decided, would make a suitable husband.

A few days later, Khadija invited Muhammad to her house and proposed marriage. Muhammad thanked Khadija for the honour and told his uncles about her proposal. His uncle Hamza went formally to her father, Khuwaylid, and the marriage was settled.

And so it was that Muhammad came to be married to the richest woman in all of Makka. They live happily together for many years.

Of course many people said that the Prophet of God had married Khadija for her wealth.

'Anyone who knew him saw that money was of no interest to him,' laughed Ka'ab, one of the Muslims who had emigrated to Madina. 'What a joke! You only have to walk into his house in Madina to see how simply he lives. And that's the man who could have been king of the Arab world if he'd wanted to.'

Salek thought of all the stories of the Prophet he had heard: of him sharing his meagre rations with people, of his simple tastes, of the hard times he endured when he and his family went to bed with little more than a morsel of food and a sip of water in their bellies. His simplicity and self-sacrifice were well known. But a question kept returning, clamouring for an answer. Were the claims of miracles and divine protection true? What was the reality?

'Could Maysara have imagined the angels?' he asked.

Ka'ab laughed his loud, ready laugh. 'Maysara had never heard of angels. These creatures were unknown to us Arabs. The people in Madina might have heard from the Christians about them. And, of course, Khadija's cousin Waraqa was a Christian. But he was a scholar and did not spend his time telling others about his beliefs.'

'But might Maysara have heard him talking about them? And could he have made a connection between the monk's remark and Waraqa's religion and conjured up the angels in his imagination?'

'I'm a simple man,' Ka'ab replied. 'I don't care for these debates about reality and imagination.'

Salek reflected on the story he had just heard. What was its essence? He thought hard. This extraordinary combination of qualities in one man showed that he was chosen by God to be special. If someone is special to God, surely God protects him in special ways. That protection may come in forms invisible to the rest of us. Salek would never know if Maysara had really seen the angels, but perhaps that did not matter.

Salek pulled himself out of his reverie. Another story was about to begin and, in the stillness around him, Salek could sense that this was an important one.

It was not often that Waraqa, the scholar, spoke. But then, it seemed right that he should be inspired to speak in the home of Sadea and Harith. It was, after all, the house of stories.

The Message

My cousin, Khadija, had been married to Muhammad for some time. They were a happy couple with a brood of children. He was a well-respected merchant who had earned himself a place in Makkan society. Beneath the calm exterior, however, was a man who was desperately seeking some sort of enlightenment and trying to find God. He was a very pious man—he meditated, fasted, prayed, gave money to the poor—but, as it turned out, he was not prepared when God decided to find him instead.

During the season when the pilgrims came to Makka in their thousands, Muhammad would move his family away from the crowded city. Until the city was emptied of pilgrims, they would stay in a cave on Mount Hira, one of the many hills overlooking Makka.

It was in AD 610, on their first night on the mountain, that

Khadija came to me. It was very late at night (or early in the morning, depending on how you look at it) when I heard banging on my door. I jumped up, wondering what it would be. I found my cousin breathless at the door.

'Waraqa!' she cried, shaking.

'Khadija! I thought you were on Mount Hira!'

'I was,' she said. 'But something has happened . . . I had to come and see you . . . I need your advice.'

She came in and sat down, and once she had calmed down a bit, she began to relate her story.

'Muhammad woke me not long ago,' she began. 'He was in a terrible state. He dragged himself to me from outside the cave, imploring me to cover him. As I did this, he began to tell me what had happened to him.' She paused and took a deep breath, still shaking.

'He told me that he had woken up in a state of terror,' she continued. 'He felt as though his whole body was gripped in a clamp. As if someone was crushing not only his body but the whole core of his being tight enough to squeeze the life out of him. He said it was as if some supernatural force—an angel—was embracing him in such a grip that his breath was being forced out of him.

'And then he heard a command—"RECITE!"

'He was terrified. He tried to explain—to whoever or whatever was issuing the order—that he could not. "I am no trained poet," he said. "I do not know anything to recite. I . . . I can't even read."

'He felt the sensation of pressure building up once more, as though the clamp was being tightened.

'"RECITE!" thundered the voice once more. "Recite in the name of your Lord who created man from a drop of blood. Recite! Your Lord is most bountiful, who by the pen taught man what he did not know."

'Muhammad heard words spill from his own mouth, coming out as easily as breath. He did not know what he was saying, or where the words were coming from. But they were pouring forth and he was powerless to control them.

'When he finally stopped, he felt the vice-like grip dissipate and it seemed we were alone once more. He panicked as he tried to make sense of what had just happened. (God forgive me, his confusion when he told me of this made me think of the ramblings of the possessed.) He became more and more convinced that he had been possessed by a spirit—a djinn. He decided—,' Khadija wiped her eyes with her trembling hands and continued in a determined manner—'that it would be best for him, for us, if he ended it there and then. He left the cave and began to make his way up the mountain.'

'Halfway up the mountain, he was stopped by a voice from the skies.

'"I looked up," he said, "and there before me, I saw the Archangel Gabriel, in the shape of a man but with extended wings . . . His feet touched the ground but he filled the sky, the whole horizon. I turned my face away from him and looked in other directions, but wherever I looked, there he was. I saw his form everywhere."

'Muhammad realized that suicide was both impossible and futile. He ran all the way back down the mountain and staggered back into the cave to tell me about his awesome experience.'

Khadija paused again and looked at me. 'Waraqa—you understand why I had to come and see you at this hour of the night. You have always been my spiritual guide. I don't know where else to turn. Please, please, help us! Explain what has happened, what is happening, to my husband . . .'

I could only confirm what she suspected. Her husband was a Prophet of God. Khadija was somewhat comforted by my words. She was as well aware as I was of the hardships that must lie ahead for a man selected by God to execute the divine will. She returned to the hills to her husband, to listen to the message he had received. And in the days that followed, she was the first to accept and acclaim him as the Prophet of Allah.

When he had recovered enough to walk, Muhammad returned to Makka. I sought him out as he visited the Ka'aba.

'It will not be easy,' I warned, my heart heavy at the thought of what must lie ahead. 'You will be forced to sacrifice what you have worked for—your position in society, your good name. You—the most honest of men—will be accused of lying; you will be persecuted, attacked, exiled, shunned and rejected.' Then I bowed before my cousin and kissed his brow. And that was how I first acknowledged the Prophet of Allah and took his message deep into my heart.

Old Waraqa's eyes sparkled with crystal tears against the silver of his eyelashes as he thumped his chest. 'How I wished that my words could have been proved wrong. But far from it. The people of Makka were up in arms. They tried to frighten Muhammad and insult him at every turn. Their leaders tortured him and his followers. And the worst among them was the man who has come to be known among Muslims as Abu Jahl, the Father of Folly.'

The Father of Folly

Amr ibn Hisham's hatred for Muhammad grew more poisonous every day. Every time he saw him, he insulted him, but the Prophet ignored him and went about his business. This annoyed Amr even more. He began to fantasize about how he would humiliate Muhammad and boasted to his friends of the terrible things he would do to bring him to his feet.

'I'll throw camel dung on his back while he's praying,' he once vowed. At other times, he came up with equally vile ideas.

One day when Amr and his cronies were sitting in the surrounds of the Ka'aba, they saw the Prophet enter. Muhammad saw them too, but as usual, he ignored their insults and walked towards the Station of Ibrahim. He said his prayers, taking his time over them, and then came out to the Ka'aba. He reached up to the black stone, the fragrant hijr-aswad embedded in the side of the Ka'aba. Then he began to circle the Ka'aba.

'He's circling the Ka'aba,' shouted Amr, 'but his mind is fixed somewhere up in the sky.'

'You don't need to remind us,' laughed a friend of Amr. 'Who is crazy enough to proclaim a God he cannot see when there are more than three hundred powerful ones inside the Ka'aba, who have helped us since time began?'

'Ah,' said someone else. 'Let the mad alone. What's the point of wasting precious time thinking about them?'

The Prophet could hear them but he did not let their nonsense interrupt his prayers.

'Ignore him?' Amr bellowed, annoyed that Muhammad was not responding. 'He is a dangerous man. He can't be ignored. He must be taught a lesson.'

He leapt to his feet and charged over to the Prophet. But Muhammad stepped out of his way and continued on his path round the Ka'aba.

'He dares to ignore me!' Amr shouted, prefacing these words with foul abuse as he returned to sit with his friends.

The men kept watching Muhammad, calling out insults and laughing loudly. But the Prophet was unperturbed. When he finished his prayers, he walked over to the hillock of Safa and knelt there.

Amr leaped to his feet again and strode aggressively up to Safa. He grabbed Muhammad's shoulders and tried to drag him to his feet. Muhammad stood up of his own accord but said nothing.

'There is no room for your religion in this city,' Amr blustered. 'Do not speak to us about this invisible God of yours who insults the gods of our ancestors.'

The Prophet towered above Amr, looking at him without uttering a word. Amr dropped his gaze and went back to his friends.

'That should get rid of him,' boasted Amr.

But Muhammad simply sat down again.

Amr was furious. 'This fellow never learns,' he shouted. 'He needs to be taught a proper lesson.'

'Who needs to be taught a lesson?' roared a loud voice. The men turned around. The words had been spoken by Abu Hamza, Muhammad's uncle.

The men were shaken. No one wanted to offend Hamza, whose sword was swifter than his tongue.

Hamza leapt off his horse and looked around at people who had gathered around.

'My hunting trip has been successful.' He stroked the

animals strapped to his horse, then raised a warning hand. 'Make sure it does not walk away while I go and thank the gods for their kindness.'

'Tsssst! Abu Hamza! Wait for me.' A woman was waving at him from her doorway. He paused, looking at her inquiringly.

'Wait a moment,' said the woman, hurrying over to him. She spoke in an urgent whisper. 'Amr ibn Hisham and his cronies have been insulting Muhammad all morning. As usual, he won't retaliate, but they just aren't letting him go about his business. Just the other week, they dumped a heap of camel dung on his back while he bowed down to pray. I can see it all, you understand. I can see the Ka'aba from my window.'

Hamza's face turned red. He clenched his fists. 'You've done well to tell me,' he rasped from between clenched teeth.

He turned and strode over to Amr ibn Hisham. 'Stand up,' he commanded.

Amr scrambled to his feet. 'At your service, Abu Hamza,' he said. 'What can I do for you?'

'The same as you've done for my nephew,' snapped Abu Hamza.

'Who? Muhammad?'

Abu Hamza grabbed Amr's robes. 'Go on,' he challenged.

'Insult me as you insult Muhammad. Have you got the courage?'

'But he offends our gods,' stammered Amr.

'But you just attack men who refuse to hit back?'

'He insults our forefathers,' Amr carried on.

'I follow his religion,' Abu Hamza said. 'I say what he says.'

The crowd was stunned. Abu Hamza, the man who worshipped the gods of the Ka'aba every day without fail, who even now—or so they thought—had come to the Ka'aba to thank the gods for their kindness, had accepted Muhammad's message of the One God!

No one knew if the Prophet's message struck Abu Hamza in that moment as he faced Amr ibn Hisham or if it had been slowly dawning on him before. But that day, he publicly made a nonsense of Amr ibn Hisham's insults and rewarded the forbearance of the Prophet. From that moment on, Muhammad and his companions had a champion in Makka that few dared to annoy.

Another Misadventure of Abu Jahl

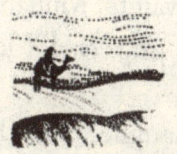

Amr Ibn Hisham's hatred for the Prophet didn't stop after that day.

'Why can you never give us any proof of your prophethood?' he demanded. 'We hear there have been prophets before you but we're told they performed amazing feats which can't be explained by logic. They walked on water and fed millions with a small amount of food, like the Christian prophet, or they made predictions about the future. What can you do to prove that your God has sent a message through you?'

'It's true,' his friends agreed. 'Why won't your God send a sign to show who you are?'

Muhammad tried to reason with the men but when they continued to insult his God, he simply got up and walked away.

Abu Jahl hated Muhammad's ability to walk away without getting embroiled in a fight. He felt his anger bubbling up. 'I will kill him,' he vowed. 'I will put an end to his trouble-making. I will find a stone so heavy that I can barely lift it. I'll take it to the Ka'aba and lie in wait for Muhammad. Then, as he bows down for his morning prayers, I'll leap out and smash his skull open.'

Abu Jahl's friends laughed and cheered. This was going to be fine sport. Encouraged by them, Abu Jahl found a large rock, hid it by the Ka'aba and waited for the Prophet to come in. Behind a screen, his friends gathered together to watch the dramatic events that were about to unfold. This was going to be more fun than the performances of the Bedouins and the stories of the poets. This was going to be a theatre of real life and death.

Walking swiftly, in his usual way, Muhammad approached his favourite space in the southern quarter by the Ka'aba and took up his position, facing Syria, with the black stone in front of him. He dropped to his knees and began praying.

Abu Jahl heaved the stone on to his shoulders and began creeping forward.

Muhammad bowed forward, prostrating himself before the Ka'aba.

Abu Jahl moved rapidly. Beads of sweat broke out on his

forehead. There was nothing now between him and his target. The muscles of his neck bulged as he strained to lift the rock up high above his head. The veins in his temple swelled and turned blue. His friends watched, hardly daring to breathe. Any moment now and . . .

Suddenly Abu Jahl turned and ran. When he reached his amazed friends, he was a ghastly shade of white and he shook and shuddered like a camel-calf caught in a hailstorm.

'What's the matter?' they muttered.

Abu Jahl's eyes bulged from his head. He was clinging to the rock so hard that his hands seemed stuck to it. He opened his mouth but no sound came out.

'What happened?' they asked again.

Abu Jahl fought to push out the words. 'The camel,' he stammered. 'The camel stallion . . .'

His friends stared at him, bewildered. 'What stallion?'

'The one that came between me and Muhammad.' He paused and his face filled with terror. 'Did you see his shoulders? And his head? And . . . and his . . . teeth?' He reeled and seemed about to fall. One of his friends caught him hurriedly.

'By God!' Abu Jahl stuttered. 'He looked as if he was determined to *eat* me!'

'They say that it was the Angel Gabriel again, come to protect the Apostle of God. But who knows if that was truth or rumour. What we do know is that Abu Jahl saw something his friends did not and it was enough to terrify him.

'By God's grace and protection, the Prophet was saved. If Abu Jahl had not been stopped by whatever vision he had, he would not have lost his best chance of finishing Muhammad off that day.'

A cheer went up in the gathering. Sadea placed fresh bread and a large bowl of yoghurt on the table, flavoured with crisp, green sprigs of mint.

'Tell me,' said Salek, leaning forward. 'Why is it that the Prophet never performed a miracle?'

'Miracles!' said Waraqa. 'Any magician or sorcerer can create a miracle. It's sleight of hand. The ability to distract with the tongue while you deceive with the hand, to conjure with the mind so that the eye is easier to fool. Magicians, you can find two a penny in any town centre on market day. Prophets are a different matter.'

'And this one was different even from the others,' Salek murmured.

Some of the gathering looked at each other. The boy was a dissenter.

'He was indeed different,' one man said. 'He brought the final message. He put paid to ideas of magic and miracle. He demonstrated that true belief has nothing to do with the fantastical.'

'Still,' Salek insisted. 'There must have been a moment when Muhammad felt his Lord could have helped him out more.'

One man walked over and sat down next to Salek. He was young and had an intense air about him. 'There was such an occasion.' He looked around at the assembly. 'I have told some of you about it before. I did not understand it and I am not in the habit of spreading tales if I do not remember every part of an event exactly as it happened. So listen carefully: my story will be brief and I can give no further explanation.' He took a deep breath. 'My name is Anas ibn Malek. Many of you will remember this line from the Quran. It is possible that it relates to the event I am about to narrate.'

The Night the Moon was Split

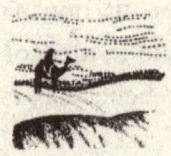

The hour of judgement is nigh, and the moon is cleft asunder.
But if they see a Sign, they turn away and say, 'This is (but)
transient magic.' (Surah 54)

'The story is set in Makka, some years before the migration
to Madina. The people of Makka came to Medina and
asked the Prophet to show them a miracle. So he pointed to
the moon and, as they looked, it split in two halves. Between
the two halves, they saw Mount Hira.'

Another man in the group nodded as Anas spoke. 'I recall
ibn Masud relating the same incident. He said that one half
of the moon remained over the mountain while the other
slipped beyond. The Prophet of God told his challengers,
"Witness this miracle."'

Anas nodded and looked over at Salek. 'Tell me, traveller, does the miracle convince you?'

Salek was embarrassed. He had achieved nothing by joining the ranks of those who had challenged Muhammad.

'Perhaps it would have,' he murmured, holding on to shreds of his pride, 'if I had seen it myself.'

Anas stood up suddenly, his face flushed. 'Remember, traveller, many people have asked me for information about the Apostle but I have never repeated anything that I am not sure of. I would never sully my record for any man. The truth is more important than the approval of a single dissenter.'

He nodded to the company, thanked Sadea for her hospitality and left.

'Perhaps,' thought Salek, still uneasy from the encounter, 'it is one of the questions I must raise with the Prophet. If I ever succeed in meeting him.'

The Night Journey

'All of them speak the truth for they only tell what they have heard.'

The Prophet did not know what had woken him. 'Alhamdu'lillah.' Praising God was second nature to him. He did it without thinking. And now, as he looked out of his window and saw the upturned, dense blue cup of the sky dusted with its billion glittering stars, he was filled with admiration and overwhelming gratitude. The surge of praise and joy he felt he could only express by repeating 'Alhamdu'lillah'. How much humankind had to thank God for.

Now that he was awake, he would go to the sacred mosque to pray. It did not matter that it was past midnight. Muhammad knew this city so well that he could have found his way blindfolded, to any part of it. Those hours he had spent as a child, playing by his grandfather's bed in the shadow of the Ka'aba, had etched the magnificent monolith and its surroundings indelibly on his mind.

He stood in its shelter now and prayed. The smooth black surface seemed to absorb the light of the moon and stars and shone with its own radiance.

A wave of drowsiness came over Muhammad as he finished praying. He fell asleep on the spot where he knelt.

Muhammad felt someone waking him. He sat up and looked around. It was Gabriel.

'Peace and blessings be upon you, Muhammad,' he said, leading the Prophet to the furthest corner of the mosque. There, standing before them was a magnificent white animal. It was larger than a donkey and yet smaller than a horse.

'This is al-buraq,' Gabriel told him. 'Mount it.'

The Prophet did as Gabriel asked. Once he was astride, the horse took off. Each of its strides was so long that it covered the entire range of human vision. In no time at all, the buraq arrived in Jerusalem and landed at the House of Holiness, the Bayt al-Muqaddas.

Muhammad dismounted and tied his mount to a ring where the prophets before him had tethered their animals.

He looked up at the mosque and once again praised God before entering and offering prayers.

When he came out again, Gabriel was waiting with two bowls. One was filled with milk and the other with wine.

'Which one will you choose?' Gabriel pointed at two bowls. The bowl of milk was cool and silvery in the moonlight and Muhammad chose it without hesitating.

Gabriel smiled. 'You have chosen the way of nature,' he said. 'Come with me.'

Together, Gabriel and the Prophet rose high into the sky. 'This is the lower heaven,' Gabriel told Muhammad as they came to a stop. He asked in a loud voice for the door to be opened.

'Who are you?' asked a voice.

'Gabriel,' the angel replied.

'And who have you brought with you?'

'Muhammad.'

'Has he received Revelation?' the voice asked.

'He has received Revelation,' Gabriel confirmed.

The door swung open. Standing in front of Muhammad was Adam, the first man in creation.

'Welcome, Muhammad,' he smiled. 'May you flourish.'

Then it was time to go. Gabriel took the Prophet higher and higher. At each heaven, he met one of the great prophets of the past: Ismail, Adam, Jesus. At the sixth heaven, he met Moses, and at the seventh, Abraham. Each one blessed him before seeing him on his way.

Now Muhammad found himself in a space beside a tree.

'This is the Lote Tree of the Furthest Limit,' Gabriel told him.

Muhammad looked at the tree. Its enormous leaves reminded him of the ears of elephants and it was studded with small fruits. As Muhammad watched, the fruits converted into objects as beautiful as the most fabulous gems.

Then God revealed many things to Muhammad, including the instruction that his followers were to offer prayers five times during each cycle of night and day.

And from that day on, the Messenger called his companions to prayer five times, beginning with the first glimmer of the sun's rays and ending when darkness brings normal activity to a close and nature begins the creation of a new dawn.

And the night during which these events took place is called the Night of M'iraj.

'You say that the Prophet, peace be upon him, gave this account himself?'

The companions nodded. A murmur went through them

as they tried to remember, among themselves, precisely which of them had been present.

'I wasn't there myself,' an old man said after a while. 'But it was Anas ibn Malek who told us—and we all know that no man is as accurate as he is. Besides, he is frequently with the Messenger.'

Salek reflected on this. If Anas was as reliable as everyone said, then perhaps he could help Salek in his quest.

'I will search him out tomorrow and ask him to take me to the Prophet,' he resolved.

Anas was blunt when Salek made his request. 'Why do you wish to meet him? Is it to ask for proof of his prophethood as you did last night?'

Salek felt uneasy under Anas's direct gaze. 'Not exactly,' he began. 'But I have to confess, I'm not exactly sure what it is I want to find out.'

Anas took pity on the young lad. There was clearly something on his mind.

'I have seen you before,' he said. 'And every time, you ask questions about our holy Prophet. It's obvious you're interested in his life.'

Salek nodded, miserably.

'Try to trust me,' Anas prompted. 'Tell me what it is you're trying to find out.'

Salek took a deep breath. 'It's a long story,' he said. 'And a sad one. If you have the time, I will explain.'

Anas listened as Salek told him how his father's mind had filled with Muhammad and his verses with stories of his life and his deeds, to the point where he neglected his father's business and his only child's welfare.

'What is your name?' Anas asked.

'I am Salek, son of . . .'

'Sa'd, the poet. The one people call al-Shair?'

Salek stared at Anas. How did this stranger know about his father?

Anas laughed softly. 'It's no magic or miracle. I met your father many times. He was, well, I suppose you could describe him as a camp follower. We'd come across him on our travels, always asking questions—just as you do now—and making careful notes of everything the Apostle of God said.'

Salek was amazed. 'He must have travelled while we were away. He never told us.'

Anas smiled. 'He hoped you would follow in his footsteps. He asked me to look out for you. He said that I should guide you but only if you asked.' He paused and looked closely at Salek's face. 'I believe your father wanted you to understand his passion for the Prophet and his words. But it was not something he could explain to you. He wanted you to understand for yourself.'

'Was my father . . . I mean, had he . . . become a Muslim?'

'I don't know if he ever acknowledged it openly,' Anas replied honestly. 'But in his heart, I am sure he did.'

'Please,' Salek begged. 'Please, Anas ibn Malek, take me to your Prophet. Let me speak to him. Let me understand my father's passion.'

Anas nodded. 'I will see what I can do. But we leave today for Madina.' He stopped short. 'Why don't you come with us? In Madina the Prophet will have more time to receive visitors and you can attend his Friday sermons. And I am sure that on the way you will hear many tales of the way Muhammad and others were forced out of Makka.'

Salek hesitated a moment. 'It is a long way.'

'The longer you can spend in the company of God's Apostle, the luckier you'll think yourself. My mother brought me to him when I was ten—only four years younger than you.

I have learned more and lived more in these ten years since than most men do in a lifetime.'

The next morning Salek thanked Harith and Sadea and joined the expedition to Madina. And just as Anas had promised, the memories of the first Muslims were rekindled by the light of the stars each night, when the fires blazed and the travellers rested beneath the desert sky.

A Traveller Recollects

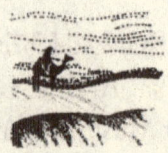

We have put a barrier before them and a barrier behind them and covered them over so that they cannot see. (Surah 36)

This story was told to me by Ali ibn Talib, Muhammad's cousin, who was one of the first of Muhammad's household to accept the holy message. They tell me Satan himself came to members of the Quraysh. He was disguised as a man of noble birth and he helped them hatch an evil plan to murder the Prophet. The Makkans were all happy to do that—but their greatest worry was that the assassin's clan would be rejected by all the others.

'If each of the seven branches of the tribe sends its strongest warrior,' said Umayyah, who was always at the forefront of any plan to destroy Muhammad, 'then no single branch can be the target of any other's vengeance.'

This plan was accepted and a day was chosen. The seven men would hide themselves around Muhammad's house during the night. When he left at dawn to say his prayers, they would surround him and kill him. If Muhammad's supporters identified them, their clans would gather in force to protect them as no one group could be held responsible.

On the very night that they planned to execute their diabolical plan, Ali told me that the Prophet was visited by the Angel Gabriel.

'Allah grants you permission to leave Makka,' he told Muhammad. 'But be warned, O Prophet, for danger awaits you if you sleep in your bed tonight.'

The Prophet understood what this meant and he told Ali the news straightaway.

'Let me sleep in your bed tonight, Prophet of God,' Ali said. 'I will wrap myself in your blanket and your enemies will not be able to distinguish between us.' Muhammad accepted Ali's offer and assured him that he would come to no harm.

In the dead of night, the Quraysh warriors crept up to the Prophet's house and hid themselves all around it. As Muhammad prepared to leave, Allah removed the sight of the seven warriors. They waited, alert for their prey, straining their eyes in the dark, while Muhammad slipped away unseen.

Inside, Ali lay awake listening for any movements.

'What are you waiting for?' a man asked the warriors as he passed outside Muhammad's house several hours later.

'For Muhammad!' they replied.

'In that case, you've got a long wait ahead of you,' chuckled the man. 'I saw him just a few hours ago and he was certainly a very long way from here.'

'That's impossible,' scoffed the warriors as the man walked on. But their suspicions were aroused. 'If Muhammad is not inside,' they vowed, 'we will hunt him down.'

From the Prophet's bed, Ali strained his ears to listen to their movements. He knew that he would come to no harm because Muhammad had promised him so—still, he could not help being a little concerned. He pulled Muhammad's cloak tightly around him and carefully covered his face. It was important that the warriors believed he was Muhammad.

The warriors shoved open the door and looked inside. They saw a man wrapped in the Prophet's blanket, sleeping peacefully. Satisfied, they crept out of the house and resumed their positions. Ali fell into a peaceful slumber.

At dawn, when Ali awoke, the warriors were still waiting. Calmly he got dressed and let himself out of the door. The warriors readied themselves to jump on him but stopped abruptly in shock.

Ali recognized the men—seven of Makka's greatest warriors. They would have to return unsuccessful to their chieftains today and admit that they had been duped by Muhammad.

There was great hilarity among the listeners who had been among the early companions.

The time before the migration from Makka had been painful and difficult for many of them, as it had been for all those who believed in Muhammad. Men like Abu Jahl and his cronies had not stopped at bullying and blustering, rather they had moved on to torture. Slaves were beaten to death, mothers were tortured before their sons, and children slaughtered as their parents watched.

At last, Muhammad received instructions from God to send the Muslims to places where they would be safe. He himself had stayed on, still trying to spread the word of God. Yet here today, Salek's travelling companions recalled the hard times with a laugh on their lips and a light in their eyes, preferring to dwell on the success rather than the wounds. Admiration welled up in Salek's heart.

In the darkness and the silence between stories, Salek heard a frail voice call his name. Moments later, an old man came and sat down facing him.

'So you are the young man who is so eager to hear the stories of our beloved Prophet. Well, I have one to tell you.'

In the light of the flames, Salek saw his eyes scan the hills on which they had set up camp. And then he began his tale.

The Flight from Makka

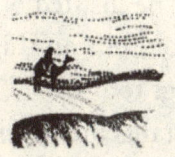

Do they not see how we have given them a sanctuary for their safety while all around them men are carried off by force?
(Surah 29)

I am Abu Bakr. I am honoured to be a close companion of Muhammad. Allah had been kind to me and I had a large house in the middle of Makka. The Prophet came straight to my house after he escaped the Quraysh warriors.

'Allah has given me permission to leave,' he said. 'We must go.'

'Together?' I asked, full of anticipation, as I had been hoping that I would be chosen to accompany him on the journey to Yathrab.

'Together.'

I was so happy to hear this that I was nearly in tears! I

had made some preparations in the preceding week or so. I had acquired two of the strongest camels. One was to be my gift to Muhammad but he insisted on buying it from me.

'I am grateful to you, but on this occasion I must only ride a camel that belongs to me.'

I had also made arrangements for Amir, a shepherd, to follow us with a flock of sheep. The sheep would obliterate the hoof prints of the camels and we would leave no trail. My son Abdullah was to come with us to the caves—there were many caves along the way and Muhammad and I planned to stop at one of them for a while. Then Abdullah would return to Makka, so that he could bring us provisions and news.

We set off for Mount Thawr, which lies to the south of Makka. It lay on the road to Yemen, away from the Yathrab route, where the Makkans would be following us. This way, we thought we could go longer unnoticed.

We managed to leave without being seen and the grace of God was with us because we were not spotted by anyone as we progressed on our trip either. When we had ridden some distance, Muhammad turned around and looked back at the city we were leaving behind.

'Upon the whole earth of Allah, you are dearest to me,

Makka,' he declared in a voice full of passion. 'If my people had not driven me out, I would not have left you.'

I looked at him and saw extreme sadness in his eyes.

We continued along the hot, dusty road until we found some caves. We examined them carefully and chose the safest one to stay in. We made sure that our tracks were covered. I instructed Abdullah to return to Makka with our camels. I felt sure he would come to no harm—the sight of men driving camels back and forth from Makka was a common one. Also, it was unlikely that there would be search parties along the way; as I said before, our pursuers were much more likely to be searching for us on the road to Yathrab.

Abdullah returned some three days later with fresh supplies and brought with him news of Makka.

'The Quraysh warriors are furious,' he exclaimed. 'They suspect you have accompanied Muhammad, Father. They came to our house and inquired about you. Of course, Ayesha told them she had no idea where you were. Then one of the brutes struck her so violently that her earring flew off.'

My son's words pierced me like a spear of pain. Like Muhammad, I felt intense grief at leaving the place which had always been my home, and I felt I should be there to protect my family. The warriors had been cowardly enough to strike my daughter, Ayesha, because they believed she was unprotected; this both saddened and enraged me.

'Search parties are coming out,' continued Abdullah. 'The Quraysh have offered a reward of one hundred camels for locating the two of you.'

I instructed him to return to Makka immediately, before the search parties exhausted the roads to Yathrab and came up the mountain.

Within a matter of days, several search parties decided to search Mount Thawr. We hid inside our cave listening. The relentless beat of footsteps came closer and closer. The questioning voices turned to excited shouts, growing louder and louder. The mountain was teeming with men and I was convinced we could not remain hidden for long.

Some warriors came up to the ledge above our cave. I felt sick. I whispered to Muhammad, 'If one of them turns around and looks under his feet, he will see us!'

He tried to comfort me. 'What do you think of two who have Allah as their third?'

The calming words sank into my heart, bringing a sense of peace. That was when something miraculous happened.

As we watched, a spider began to spin a web across the opening of the cave. We watched it work—I have never seen anything so fast, or so skilful—as it wove its glistening silver thread, building a veil that stretched across the width of the entrance from one side to the other.

I could see for sure that Allah was protecting us. I began to believe that we could go unnoticed. I had never been so aware of divine intervention.

And then there was one more amazing event. Two pigeons quickly gathered twigs and branches from a nearby tree and built a nest in the corner of the entrance. As the men clambered down from the ledge and made towards the entrance of the cave, the female pigeon settled into the nest and laid some eggs.

The substantial web and the nest filled with eggs made it look that the mouth of the cave had been undisturbed for quite some time. But I was still afraid that the search party might try to gaze through the web and catch sight of us inside. So the Prophet and I retreated as far back into the cave as possible.

'We've missed a cave over here!' yelled one man.

From the thundering footsteps I could tell that several members of the search party were headed our way.

'Fool,' yelled a different voice. 'Look at the size of this spider's web. It would have been hanging in shreds if someone had entered this cave.'

'And that pigeon,' added another. 'She wouldn't build her nest in a cave occupied by humans. There's no point wasting time here.'

'Are you sure?' persisted the man who had first drawn attention to our hideout.

I stayed as still as I could, afraid even to breathe in case they heard me.

'Absolutely sure.'

And with that, we heard the footsteps retreating.

Abu Bakr pointed across at some hills. 'There is Mount Thawr, the place where all nature joined together to do the will of God. And I was blessed enough to see it.'

Two young men came forward, their faces glowing in the firelight. Salek knew they were called Sal and Suhayl. They, too, had a story to tell. Sal began—

A Divine Choice

Word quickly reached us in Yathrab that Muhammad and Abu Bakr had arrived in Quba, a suburb of the city. They had been warmly received with much rejoicing. Women and children sang a welcome song they had composed.

Muhammad lodged there for three days. The people asked the Prophet to tell them where they should build their mosque. He looked at the eager faces around him, each one was filled with hope that Muhammad would choose his land for the honour. Whichever spot he chose, he was bound to disappoint the others. As usual, he asked God for guidance, and when he had received it, he responded.

'I will allow my camel Kaswa to wander. Wherever she rests, there we will build our mosque.'

The camel was given free reign and she chose the spot. Work on the Mosque of Quba began immediately.

Just as news of the Prophet's arrival reached us, news of us reached the Prophet. We, the people of Yathrab, anxiously awaited him.

Very shortly afterwards, he left his temporary home in Quba and journeyed into our city, accompanied by a large party.

We remember waiting for them to arrive, listening for every movement, hearing the faraway rhythm of camel hooves on the ground grow closer and closer. We were practically silent as we strained our ears in breathless anticipation. We remember scanning the huge group of newly arrived men, trying to identify the Prophet. It was not difficult—there was something fresh and radiant about him, even after his hardships and many days spent travelling. He seemed unaffected by the heat but lit by a glow from within.

Muhammad led us in the first Friday prayer at his new home and we rejoiced at his presence among us. As he passed through the crowds after the prayer, greeting his followers, many people opened their doors for him. He refused everyone politely—even relatives of his mother who he recognized. Once again, he decided to live where Kaswa sat down.

I wished more than anything to offer him a place to live. But all I possessed was a small plot of land which my brother and I owned. It contained date trees and a building that had fallen into disrepair, as well as a modest prayer area set up by Asad, our foster father. It would be an insult to expect the Holy Messenger of Allah to stay in such a dilapidated house.

The camel continued past the Prophet's relatives' and ten, twenty, thirty other homes. Imagine my shock when it ambled on to our land!

I felt the blood rush to my cheeks. I waited for Kaswa and Muhammad to ride on through the small courtyard and on to the next place. Instead, Kaswa walked slowly to our makeshift prayer area and knelt down. Muhammad let go of the reins.

I squeezed my brother's hand and we held our breath.

Kaswa got up and walked around the courtyard once more. She returned to the spot where she had knelt and bent down once again, settling herself on the ground.

There was silence for a minute. Then the Prophet announced, 'If it is Allah's will—this will be my home! Who owns it?'

'It belongs to the two orphaned boys,' called someone from the crowd.

'Sal and Suhayl! Asad's boys,' called someone else.

The Prophet smiled. 'Will someone bring them to me?'

Suhayl and I stepped forward, our hearts thudding, unable to believe that this was truly happening.

The Prophet smiled again. 'Can I buy this land from you?'

'Oh, no,' I said. 'You can have the land just like this, O Holy Messenger.'

'Please,' added Suhayl, 'accept it as a gift.'

The Prophet seemed pleased at our offer, but refused to accept it for free and later negotiated a price with Asad, our foster father. And from then on, our small plot of land became his home. And our city of Yathrab gained fame throughout the Arab world as the Madina, *the* City.

It was not long before the travellers entered the famous city of Madina. There was a quickness in Salek's step and a lightness in his heart as he looked around him. Many of his companions offered him shelter. For the first time in his life, Salek felt he could happily have stayed with any of these people without fear of being exploited. He realized, surprised, that he trusted them.

'You will stay with me,' Anas told him. 'But first we will go the house of the Prophet and see that he has all he needs.'

Eagerly, Salek followed Anas until they came to a house

which was not much more than a hut. Salek gaped, amazed, at the walls of unbaked clay holding up a roof of palm-thatching covered by camel skin.

Anas led him inside and looked around. Someone had cleaned the room. The floor had been swept and the animal skin on the floor dusted. On the rope bed, the leaf-filled mattress and pillow had both become flat from many years of use.

'We have suggested many times to change the mattress,' Anas said, 'but the Prophet says he has no need of such comforts.' He walked over to the other side of the bed and picked up a leather water bag. 'I will bring him some fresh water.'

As they walked out the house, Anas paused in front of Salek for a moment. 'Tomorrow, you will meet the Prophet.'

Salek's heart leapt. As he followed Anas, he smiled quietly to himself. He was filled with a strange sense of calm. The feeling of despair, the fiery resentment, the tension of confrontation that had filled him before, at the thought of this momentous event, were no longer there.

Salek saw Anas scrutinizing him as he stooped to fill the water bag. 'I see your anger has gone.' His voice was quiet. 'Perhaps you have begun to understand your father better.'

Salek realized with a thrill that Anas was right.

Anas continued. 'Tonight,' he said, 'you will meet a friend of your father. He will tell a story to honour your father.'

The rest of the day sped past as people greeted their families. A big feast was prepared for the travellers who had returned. For the first time in his life, Salek had a sense of belonging as he joined in with the preparations.

And when the work was done, it was time to rest and feast their minds on another story, full of meaning and memory, from a master storyteller.

Two Holy Battles

Through the life of every man and woman stalks a shadow. And it casts itself wide and it digs itself deep through their thoughts and their doings so that there is no reprieve from it. It was no different for Muhammad, peace be upon him. Yes, you may smile. You are thinking, aren't you, that a prophet has many such enemies? And of course he did. The whole town of Makka united against him. Why else did he migrate to Madina? But my story is not about the many, it is not about the migration. It is the story of battles fought in the middle of deserts—battles that were not simply men of arms fighting their equals. It was a fight in which Right and Wrong came down to take sides.

Ah! You are thinking Muhammad's shadow was an enemy from the Makkan side! But no, you are wrong. It was a leader of Makka, certainly. Abu Sufyan? Wrong again. It was Hind, the most powerful woman in the Hijab, daughter of Utbah and wife of Abu Sufyan.

She was tall and beautiful in a strong, wild way. They say the wildness of a face reflects the wildness of its owner's nature. And Hind, people said, had the soul of a beast of prey. How do I know, you ask? All I can say in reply is that a storyteller hears and he tells. The proof and the hidden meaning are not my concern. It is my business to listen and pass on, yours to listen and do with it as you will. And here, now, is my story. I hope you, too, will pass it on.

Hind was full of hate. She was a religious woman, devoted to the worship of the gods in the Ka'aba. She paid her respects daily and she made sacrifices to them. And why shouldn't she? Since the day she was born, they showered blessings on her, gave her riches and made it possible for her to be a queen among women.

But now Muhammad, this Messenger of God, was undermining the life she loved. He declared that there was only one God, and that God was not among those housed in the Ka'aba. Even if the citizens of Ka'aba accepted this God of Muhammad and wanted to pay him respect, they would not be allowed to cast him in gold or stone and give him a place of honour. Because, Muhammad said, it was forbidden to make images of Him.

'Accepting Muhammad's message is accepting disaster!' stormed Hind. So much of the wealth of Makka came from the thousands of pilgrims who arrived here throughout the year to pay their respects to the gods of the Ka'aba, and especially the greater and lesser pilgrimages.

So you see, my friends, my patrons, my audience, Hind was not just insulted for her gods, she was worried for her wealth, her power, her position.

And yes, there was another reason. Muhammad had enchanted and entrapped her own brother. He was now in Makka and it hurt Hind to see Utbah, her father, broken-hearted. So, every minute of every day, she goaded Abu Sufyan and Utbah and her other brother Waleed. 'Make war on Muhammad. Do what you must. Bring him down.'

She looked out at Abu Bakr's shop, towering in the centre of Makka. 'Why should he benefit from the bounty of Makka when he is so bent on destroying us? Can we tolerate the man who went to Madina with Muhammad?' Hind looked at her husband, full of evil intent.

'But his son Abdullah will fight hard to protect their father's property—and his sister Ayesha.'

'I heard that Abu Bakr bought Makka's best camels to help Muhammad escape. Will he continue to plunder our best goods to use against us?'

Abu Sufyan decided it was time to act.

Within moments, his men gathered around Abu Bakr's shop. They battered down the door and burst in, helping themselves to all the goods inside. Then they swarmed through the streets and lanes of Makka, looking for other Muslim homes and shops. They broke in, threw families out into the night—there was no mercy for the old and the sick, no thought for mothers and babies—and denuded the properties of money and all valuables.

The leaders of Makka claimed all these properties, the silver goods and tapestries and jewellery and put them up for sale. Along with the cash they collected, the sale of the goods raised a mountain of money. Abu Sufyan and the others put it towards the merchandise that would go to the north. The Muslim cargo would expand their fortunes.

That night Hind hosted a massive feast. All the leaders of

Makka and their men gathered to eat and drink and dance. Let Muhammad's companions rot in the dark streets. Let them ask their God for help. Soon their caravans would leave Makka, creaking with riches.

And as they made merry, the news flew ahead of the caravans like grains of sand on the desert wind. In Yathrab, Abu Bakr was told, 'Your shop is gone! Destroyed!'

Abu Bakr shook his head, resigned. If it had not happened now, it would have happened another day. A shop was a pile of bricks and sand. It could be replaced. But it grieved him to think of people being treated in that way. 'We must find a way of helping them,' he decided, and Muhammad agreed.

But Hamza's heart was heavy. As a warrior, he had always considered the sword his best friend. He loved and respected his nephew above anyone alive, but he felt it was time to speak up against oppression. 'We have to answer their challenge,' he said to Muhammad. 'We must not let them get away with this. They may be richer but we have right on our side.'

The Prophet could understand what his uncle was saying, but war was not the answer. He reminded Hamza that Allah showed the way of peace.

Hamza said no more, but his heart felt as if the heat of the entire desert had come to rest in it and that it would surely explode if he did nothing.

And then, as if by a miracle, the message came to Muhammad in a dream. God had sanctioned war but He also laid down laws of compassion, morality and good behaviour for His soldiers to obey. At last, the Muslims were allowed to defend their principles and their property and to counter the oppression and injustice they had encountered.

'Allah-o-Akbar!' Hamza stood up in joy. 'Thank you for giving us the opportunity to show that our God is on the side of the weak and the poor as long as they are in the right.'

Imagine, for a moment, the blue dome of the desert sky, growing white behind the fierce dazzle of the sun. Beneath it, sun-like glory shines on the faces of three hundred men and a few more as they stand in front of a group of wells at Badr. For miles to the right and left of them, there is nothing but vast stretches of desert, rising and falling dune before dune, like a million waves.

'You remember the rules of God,' says the Prophet. 'You fight in His name and not for private glory or personal revenge.

These things may come to the honest warrior but he must not seek them.'

The Prophet turns to Hamza, who the companions call the Lion of God. The men raise their arms and their voices. Their spears jostle against one another. Their breath comes in excited gasps. 'Allah-o-Akbar,' they cry out together. Their collective voices become a lion's roar, echoing in the sky-dome, bouncing along the dunes. 'Allah-o-Akbar.'

'God is indeed great,' Hamza says. 'The Makkans have three men to every one of us. But we need not fear. We are fighting in the way of God. We have water to quench our thirst and wash our wounds.' Here he pauses before commanding, 'Archers at the front; spears behind them; swords at the rear.' At these curt words, the men arrange themselves into three rows. They prepare to surge forward but Hamza raises his hand. 'We will stand,' he says. 'We will wait.'

The horizon begins to curdle with smudges of thick dust-clouds. They blur the infinite line dividing sky and sand before bursting their seams and swirling upwards in dense, black puffs. Through them, the silhouettes of horsemen loom. At first, they seem like a mirage or some ghostly manifestation, for the horses run yet seem to stay on the same spot. Then comes the strange sound of hooves on sand—*thud-thud-thud*. It sounds almost like rain, but not quite.

And here they are, pounding down towards the three rows of warriors from Yathrab.

The first riders of the Makkan cavalry stop some hundred yards from the wells. But the movement of dust and riders behind them continues for some time, widening and lengthening. Their ranks swell with a massive infantry, more horses and camel.

The Muslims are full of courage. They may not have the horses or the camels or the weapons, but their hearts well with valour and their minds are full of God. In obedience to Hamza's command, they wait. They watch.

In the front row of the Makkan army, three men dismount. They stride forward, bold and forceful.

'Hamza,' says Utbah ibn Rabiah. 'Send us our equals.' He swaggers a little. 'You know me. And perhaps these famous warriors too. My brother Shaiba and my son Waleed. Have you got warriors who can match these?'

Hamza feels Muhammad's restraining arm on his shoulder and controls his anger. Calmness and precision are essential for victory. The Prophet has asked him to ensure that the first to risk their lives would be their kinsmen. It was always his way to lead by example and be the first in dangerous ventures.

'Obeida al Harith, Ali ibn Talib and I.'

The three men from Yathrab march towards the three men from Makka, who lunge forward, swords flailing. Metal rings against metal. The thrusting and parrying continues for a while. The men are well matched. Then Hamza thrusts and stands back. Utbah falls to the ground.

The Makkan army gasps as one.

Waleed turns to see his father dead on the ground. 'Watch out!' a few soldiers call.

Ali could have killed Waleed in that moment of intense emotion when his guard was down. But he holds back, for he does not wish to take unfair advantage of a man's loss.

Waleed turns back to Ali. His eyes flash poison and fury. 'Your people killed my father. You will die. You will all die like the beggars you are.' He thrusts and flails his sword, wildly, at Ali.

Ali dodges its path and waits. At the right moment, his sword rises, flashes, runs Waleed through.

A cry goes up from the Makkan side. Another warrior lost.

At the far side, the duel between Obeida and Shaiba continues. The Makkans cheer their man. 'Shaiba!'

Shaiba knows the honour of the Makkans rests on his shoulders. He brings down his sword hard on Obeida's shoulder. Obeida staggers. The Muslims can see he is severely wounded.

Hamza knows that he and Ali are entitled to help Obeida. When single combatants defeat their assailants, the rules of warfare allow their fellow fighters to assist. But Obeida is holding his own despite the blood pouring from his shoulder. Hamza and Ali move forward to take over. But before they reach him, Obeida has pulled himself together and brought Shaiba down.

The three men withdraw in respect for the dead men. The Makkans rush forward to reclaim the bodies.

A ripple runs through the three rows of Muslim fighters. They are ready, impatient to hear Hamza's command and surge forward to meet the cavalrymen from Makka. But Hamza holds up his hand in silence.

The Makkan riders advance, spears held forward.

Still there is no sign from Hamza.

The Muslims want to fight. They do not care that they

might be trampled down by enemy horses. They imagine themselves weaving between the riders, pulling them off their horses, forcing them into fair and equal combat.

Still Hamza says nothing.

Suddenly his voice cracks out. 'Archers, strike!'

The archers raise their bows, tighten their arrows and let go. A hundred arrows meet a hundred targets. Through the clouds of dust, riderless horses emerge, scattering in all directions. The remaining cavalrymen flood towards the Muslim fighters.

Again, the archers strike. More men fall. Those who remain continue their advance, supported now by hundreds of warriors on foot.

Hamza calls out another command. A barrage of spears flies out, bringing down more men. In the Muslim ranks too, men fall. They are running out of ammunition but they stand fast, ready to fight with everything they've got.

With the scrabbling of horse-hooves, the dust curtain swirls. Hamza is baffled for a moment, for he can see only the movement. Then suddenly, he distinguishes the cause of the dust-storm. The Makkan fighters have turned their horses around.

'They're retreating!' Hamza shouts. 'Hold back, men.'

A massive cheer goes up from the rows of Muslims. Their exhaustion vanishes, their wounds suddenly cease to ache.

The Muslims offer thanks to God and rejoice.

When the Makkan soldiers imprisoned by the Muslims return to Makka, they say that the Muslim army has rigid rules—prisoners must be treated with justice and fairness. 'They freed us,' the men report to Abu Sufyan, 'because each of us taught ten of their men to read and write.'

Hind listened, coiled like a serpent. Grief and anger were fighting inside her like wild animals.

'They are kind to their prisoners,' the men continued. 'That's why some accepted the message of Muhammad's God and stayed back in Yathrab.'

Hind's fury snapped her self-control and she sprang forward, scratching and clawing at the men. 'You stood back and watched my father and brother get killed,' she snarled. 'And now you tell me how Muhammad won over the people of Makka with his wheedling ways? Do you understand how I feel?'

Abu Sufyan hastily signalled the soldiers to leave.

Hind paced up and down the room, clawing at her tangled hair, spitting and frothing, swearing revenge. 'Look out for me, Hamza. I will drink your blood. I will split you open from end to end and I will eat your heart. Make no mistake. I mean every word.'

As the weeks rolled on, Hind's obsession grew deeper. And Abu Sufyan could see similar despair and hatred reflected in the eyes of all the leaders of Makka. He knew there was only one thing to do. The people of Makka had to return and fight Muhammad again.

'This time we must be prepared. We cannot assume that we can beat them just because there are more of us. We may have more weapons but they are skilled fighters,' he declared at a gathering of the leaders.

'Our fighters are just as able,' argued Khalid bin Waleed, a fiery young general. 'But I'm told the Muslims have this strange light in their eye.'

'I have seen it,' a veteran from Badr shuddered. 'It is as if they believe that a secret force is on their side.'

'Enough of all this,' Abu Sufyan snapped. 'We are talking ourselves into defeat even before we get started. I say we prepare well and win. Call up the best fighters. Tell them money is no object. Abu Sufyan will give them all they ask for to put together the best army that Arabia has ever seen.'

Now, my friends, my patrons, my providers, let me take you across a stretch of desert to the other side.

The night is soft. As the fragrance of the palms and the softly turned earth wafts into the homes of the sleepers in Yathrab, Muhammad stirs, watching the night-theatre of his dreams. The Prophet of God is standing dressed in his armour. In front of him are several heads of slaughtered cattle.

The next morning, the Prophet of God spoke to his companions. 'I had a dream last night. Abu Sufyan and the men of Makka are planning to attack us in the town of Yathrab. I believe one of my clan will be killed in battle.'

'Then let us fight,' shouted the young hotheads. 'We beat them once. We can beat them twice.'

'And as many times more as they want to be beaten,' added some others.

The Prophet shook his head. 'We must not provoke an attack or start a fight,' he advised. 'We will wait in the city. If they want to fight, let them come to us.'

'What? Into the city?' The people were incredulous.

Hamza watched their faces. If *they* were so shocked, then how much more taken aback the army from Makka would be. 'They are preparing for a fight in the open desert,' he thought. 'They will not be equipped to fight inside a city. The siege cannot last very long.'

'We prepare,' Muhammad said, 'and we wait.'

But the people wanted to meet the army from Makka out in the battlefield. 'They will think we are cowards, hiding in our homes, waiting to let them into our city and destroy it.'

'But they will find out soon enough that we are lions,' Hamza argued. 'We will prove we have prepared for battle and are willing to lay down our lives.'

Abu Bakr could see that the young men were unhappy. 'We must create an example,' he reminded them. 'We believe in peace. We only fight if there is no other way and we are forced.'

Abdullah ibn Ubayy ibn Salul, a chief of Yathrab, spoke up. 'We do not want to attack first. But if an army has travelled all the way from Makka, we know they are coming to fight us. We should go out to meet them. No one can accuse us of being the first into battle.' Many shouted in agreement.

As always, Muhammad accepted the decision of the majority. He gave the word and an army began to gather.

But even as they came together, doubt crept into some hearts. 'Perhaps the Messenger of God is right,' they said. 'We should fight from inside the city.'

But Muhammad said they must remain committed to their decision. 'Once a Prophet has put on his coat of mail,' he said, 'it is not appropriate to take it off.'

So it was, that some while later, an army of one thousand Muslims made their way out from Yathrab to the foot of a hill called Uhud. What they lacked in numbers and equipment, they made up for in morale and high spirits. This time they had a cavalry and three times the men they had at Badr. And once again, God was on their side. They chanted prayers and sang songs of courage and faith and they marched energetically.

Suddenly, a loud cry went up. The army halted.

Ibn Salul rode up to the front. 'My men and I are returning to Yathrab,' he announced. 'We have decided not to fight.'

'You won't fight?' Hamza growled. 'What made you change your mind at this hour?'

'I don't have to explain anything to you or anyone else,' Ibn Salul turned his horse around. 'We volunteered of our own free will and we are free to change our mind.'

'Are all your men going back with you?'

'Of course.' Ibn Salul was already galloping away.

The warriors watched in confusion as three hundred of their companions abandoned them.

'Perhaps they are aware of something terrible,' some men murmured. 'Perhaps we should go back with them.' But they looked around at the sad faces of their companions and decided to stay.

Hamza and the Prophet did all they could to revive the spirits of their men. The seven hundred remaining Muslims continued on their journey. But there was less energy in their marching now and less vigour in their voices. A rumour began to flutter through the ranks that Ibn Salul and his men had planned this betrayal. He had, the word was, made a deal with the men from Makka.

Hamza and the Prophet had no time for gossip. They urged the army to focus on the job before them. 'We are still more than twice the number we were at Badr,' they reminded the men. 'We have planned better and we have a cavalry.'

Hamza called them to a halt when they arrived at last at Uhud. A quick reconnoitre told him that with the mountain behind them they would need minimal defences from the rear.

But there was one small flaw in the secure wall of protection the mountain provided: a single mountain pass which could provide an opportunity for attack.

'The Quraysh army will approach from front,' Hamza said. 'If we cover that mountain pass, we should be safe.'

'Fifty archers will cover the pass,' the Prophet said. The men jumped to his command. The Prophet told them to take their positions and stand firm. 'Come what may,' he said, 'do not abandon your posts—not even if you see the birds fly off with our flesh.'

The Prophet held up a sword to the rest of the army. 'Who is willing to take this sword in return for its due?'

Enthusiasm rippled through the crowd as the sword glinted in the sun. One of the soldiers moved forward. 'What is its due, Messenger of God?' he asked.

'Abu Dujana,' Muhammad greeted the man, 'the sword's due is that you fight with it until it is broken.'

Abu Dujana bowed his head and held out his arm. 'I will pay its due,' he said.

He and others prayed for strength, courage and the chance to defeat the powerful enemy soldiers. They begged God to forgive them for past mistakes.

The army had regained its courage. The men were ready to face the enemy.

And here comes the enemy. An impressive array, the thundering of hooves as loud as the beat of their drums, weapons shining through the swirls of dust. An army of no less than three thousand men, accompanied by horses and camels laden with reinforcements of food, water and weapons.

But what the Muslims lack in men and animals and possessions, they make up for in spirit and valour. And the lines from their Book are their mighty shield:

'And many a Prophet there was, with whom a large number of God-devoted men fought. They fainted not for anything that befell them in the way of God, neither weakened nor abased themselves. God loves the steadfast. Nothing else did they say but: "Our Master, forgive our sins, and that we exceeded in our affair. Make our feet firm, and help us against the unbelievers." God gave them the reward of the world and the good reward of the hereafter. God loves those who do good.'

The battle begins! The Muslims lunge in, led by the heroes of the first war at Badr, Ali ibn Talib and Hamza. How they fly into battle, crying 'Allah-o-Akbar!' Their cries resonate and magnify so that the enemy think they are at least twice the actual number.

The two cavalries clash in a clatter of weapons.

Zubayr ibn Awwam of the Muslims valiantly fights the canny Khalid bin Waleed from Makka, each man aware of the finely honed skills of the other. Ibn Awwam is struck from behind and turns his attention to his attacker.

Immediately Waleed looks to the mountain behind. Surely there is a weakness somewhere, a spot which would provide the opportunity for him and a few men to surprise the Muslim army from the rear. A row of archers is defending the pass from an advantageous position. He cannot risk the lives of his men, but he can wait and watch.

A moment will surely come when the Muslims will call on the archers to help on the field. He watches, frustrated, as Ali fells one man after another. Hamza, the fearless warrior, is magnificent to observe. They are fighting fiercely, though they are so hugely outnumbered that one man is taking on four.

Abu Dujana, wielding a handsome sword, is stunned to find himself facing a woman. Hind snarls and spits like a crazed witch, challenging him to fight her. But he turns away to preserve the honour of the sword by fighting someone equal to its strength.

Now the eye of every warrior on foot is on Wahshi, a giant Abyssinian who weaves in and out of the warring mass, mowing down every man in his way. Two or three times, he wends his way towards Hamza but is waylaid by some other warrior determined to pit his strength against him. But no one can match his power or skill and he moves on.

Despite Wahshi's efforts, the battle belongs to the Muslims. The Makkans realize it and begin to take flight, leaving a trail of weapons, food and water. The Muslim soldiers gather the spoils.

The archers guarding the pass watch the Makkans retreat. 'God has helped us defeat the army! Look, our companions are chasing them away!'

'The war is over. We've won. Let's join our brothers.'

'We deserve our share of the rewards,' yell a few of the archers. 'The battle is over. Let's go.'

'The Prophet commanded us to stay here,' says Ibn Awwam. 'We cannot abandon our post.'

But greed overcomes some of the archers and they slide and scrabble down the slopes and across the enemy lines to get their hands on the booty. The mountain pass is largely unprotected.

Khalid bin Waleed silently signals his men to approach the undefended pass from behind the dunes.

Ibn Awwam hears the thudding of hooves on the sand. The next moment he is facing Waleed. He and his remaining handful of archers fight valiantly but they are easily overpowered.

Waleed leads his men through the pass, shouting loudly to the fleeing Makkan army to return. By the time the shocked Muslims regain their wits and turn to defend themselves, the Makkan army returns and attacks. The scattered Muslim army is under attack on both fronts.

'Get Muhammad,' shouts a Makkan commander.

The soldiers press in towards Muhammad from all sides, attacking by every means. The Prophet is wounded and his men fight with everything they have. Hamza stands in front of the Prophet, challenging anyone who approaches.

From the distance, Hind sees Hamza. She notes how he stands guarding his beloved nephew, unconcerned about his own life.

'Wahshi,' she hisses, summoning the Abyssinian warrior. 'That is the man I want. Kill him and you will be a free man— and a rich one.'

Wahshi raises his spear to his shoulder. He narrows his eyes and positions the point of his weapon precisely. With a smooth movement of his arm, he throws it—throws it to regain his freedom. His spear sails through the air and lodges itself firmly in Hamza's thigh.

Hamza falters. All around him, the Muslims fight with renewed energy. But Hamza staggers and falls dead to the ground.

Abu Sufyan has achieved his goal. Hind has her revenge.

With a flourish, the storyteller bowed and wished the group good night.

In the deep of the night, Salek awoke with a shock. He could hear his father's voice resonate in his ears. 'Read my verses. They are my legacy to you.' Why should these words come to him *now*? He thought back to Anas ibn Malek's words: 'He hoped you would follow in his footsteps . . . your father wanted you to understand his passion for the Prophet . . . He wanted you to understand for yourself.'

Salek leapt out of bed and scrabbled through his possessions for the sheaf of verses. 'At last,' he thought, 'at long last, I can try to fulfil my father's wish. I am ready to read.'

The Expedition to Makka—
Al-Shair's Ode

That day, a surge of grief rippled the desert sands. Black, tear-filled clouds, like the grieving heart of heaven, pressed down towards the desert floor. The cloud-riders were none but the black-clad men from the tribe of Khozaa, and the racing dunes, their golden camels. Forty golden dunes rose in unison to provide the clouds with a mount. Yes, it was a miracle to behold! For the next moment, these grief-filled crowds gripped the dunes and sped across the desert. Their destination Yathrab, their mission recompense. And who would be a more just and able helper than Muhammad, Messenger of God?

The citizens of Yathrab must have seen them approach from a distance, seen the golden sand kicked up by the heels of the desert ships into swirling whirls of sterile cloud. They must have seen the burning, beating sunrays search out the point and blade of sword and dagger and make them glint like threats studding the route all the way from Yathrab to Makka.

'An injustice has been done!' the leader of the Khozaa group said, grasping the hand of the Prophet, placing it against his grieving breast. 'The Bani Bakr came in the night. They used the terms of the truce as a blanket to cover their treachery. They killed our men as they slept.'

The Messenger of God rose to his feet, his eyes flashing, his face ablaze with passion. 'The truce has been violated. People have been killed. Lives lost in the darkness of the night.' For Muhammad, peace was precious and sacred, but he wanted to make sure no one compounded the evil by causing more murder and bloodshed. 'Why did they do this? Did a member of the Khozaa cast the first stone?'

Forty Khozaa voices, grained with sand, burdened with grief resounded, 'We did not!'

'Then how do you explain it?'

'Old hatred. Past enmity. The Bani Bakr and the Khozaa had many scores to settle. They could not let it go in spite of the truce in Makka.'

'Then,' the Prophet announced, 'we must go to Makka.

Abu Sufyan and the leaders of Makka promised they would lay to rest old enmities. We have to enforce promises. One who condones cruelty is as bad as one who inflicts it.'

A dark cloud strayed on to the bright sky above, shedding rain in the sun-lit heavens.

The Prophet looked up and saw the cloud. He thought of his beloved birthplace, the city which housed the sacred Ka'aba. When, O city of holiness, will the Lord grant you peace and serenity? When will you be cleansed of corruption and hostility? A sad, long sigh escaped his lips. 'Just as rain pours from that cloud, comfort will come to the Khozaa from above.'

Forty hearts were filled with gratitude. Muhammad would help them.

At that moment, the leaders of Makka are thinking of Muhammad. They know it is simply a matter of time before he hears how the Bani Bakr ambushed and slaughtered the Khozaa in the night. And then what—war? The Bani Bakr are friends of the Quraysh of Makka who resent Muhammad and his followers; the Khozaa have allied themselves with the Muslims. Muhammad dislikes broken promises as much as he hates treachery and deceit. They know he will not stand by and allow such injustice.

'Go,' they tell their chief Abu Sufyan. 'Go to Yathrab and find out what Muhammad intends.'

In Yathrab, Abu Sufyan goes to his daughter's house. Umm Habiba is married to Muhammad. Through his daughter he has direct access to this great Prophet.

Umm Habiba receives her father politely but there is no warmth in her greeting, no smile on her face. As he is about to sit, she draws away the carpet. She folds it and puts it to one side.

Abu Sufyan is puzzled. 'I don't understand, daughter,' he says, trying to make light of the insult. 'Is the carpet too good for me? Or then again, am *I* too good for the carpet?'

Still, no smile lights up Umm Habiba's face. 'It is the Prophet's carpet. I cannot let a spy sit on it.'

Abu Sufyan is offended. 'You have changed for the worst since you left me,' he snaps and leaves.

But he does not abandon his mission. He walks around the town, looking to his left and his right and all the space between, keeping his eyes open, his ears alert, for any reaction

to the complaint of the Khozaa, any plans for retaliation. He
sees nothing. He hears less than nothing. He visits Omar,
one of the Prophet's closest companions. But Omar turns
him away.

The Prophet's cousin and son-in-law was once one of Abu
Sufyan's friends. Today he is one of Muhammad's four closest
companions.

Abu Sufyan makes his way to Ali's house. 'I want to speak
to Muhammad,' he says.

'Why?' Ali is with his wife, Fatima, daughter of the Prophet,
watching as their son Hassan learns to crawl.

'I come to ask for peace. Speak to the Prophet for me,' says
Abu Sufyan. 'Don't let me return to Makka unsuccessful in
my mission of peace.'

'When the Prophet of God is occupied,' Ali replies, 'there
is no point in approaching him.'

Occupied? This does not sound good to Abu Sufyan.
Occupied with what? Thoughts of attacking Makka to punish
the breakers of the truce?

Abu Sufyan turns to Fatima. 'Let your little boy Hassan
be the guardian of peace,' he says, 'and he will be the Lord of
the Arabs for all time.'

Fatima is amazed at Abu Sufyan's impertinence.

Abu Sufyan turns again to Ali. 'What shall I do?'

'All that you can do,' replies Ali, 'is to tell the people that you guarantee protection to all as you promised at the truce.'

'Will it help?'

'I cannot say,' Ali replied honestly. 'But what else can you do?'

'But,' say the hardened leaders of Makka when Abu Sufyan relates his experience of Madina. 'Did Muhammad accept your guarantee?'

Abu Sufyan shakes his head. 'Muhammad did not speak a single word to me while I was there.'

Away in Yathrab, the Prophet of God maintained his silence. As he built his army, as he planned his moves, silence became his most astute strategy. No one must know his plans. And if no one knew, then no one would speak and if no one spoke, the plan would remain simple and direct, and above all, it would stay within the circles that generated it.

But a whispered message spread to the Bedouins in the desert. 'Join us at Madina. Or join us on the way.' And promises were carried back on chains of air, invisible, inaudible, invincible.

At last it was time. The Prophet called his men to arms. 'Get ready to go to Makka. We are fighting.' Secrecy was still Muhammad's strongest weapon. 'Go about your tasks. Get yourselves ready. Say nothing to anyone.'

But we all have fathers, wives, brothers and sons. And secrets mingle as breath and blood and they travel in the air like germs carried on vapour. And at last they go to those who must not hear. Such a carrier was Hatib.

'Go to Makka,' he said to his messenger. 'I must warn my family that the Prophet of God is coming to Makka with a powerful army.' He thrust a note at his messenger. 'Hide it well and go swiftly.'

Hatib was confident his message would be conveyed efficiently. He had chosen his messenger carefully and cunningly. The messenger tucked the message in her long, glossy locks. Who would ever guess that a woman could be a messenger?

She leaped on her horse, nimble as the breeze, and set off as Bilal's voice filled the city, calling the faithful to evening prayer. The Muslims dropped the business at hand and made their way to the mosque. As she moved out of the sight of the city gates, she glanced back quickly. No one was coming behind her. She had chosen her moment well.

She was an experienced rider and she knew her route well. The stars had often been her guide through night-rides. Her father had trained her with his compass and the study of the stars.

She felt the ground grow soft beneath her horse's hooves and knew she was in the desert. The air was still, soft and moist. The only breeze against her skin was created by her own movements.

As the night grew in darkness and length, the air became crisp and dry. Silence embraced her, holding her close and safe. She knew that the darkness of the desert could conceal others as it concealed her. The growing chill told her that she was getting deeper and deeper into the desert's heart.

She cast her eye up at the stars and saw the Seven Sisters, the poles. They indicated she was much, much further along than she had thought. She had come into the boundless spaces where only trust and faith were the friends of the traveller. And did she have any unknown companions travelling alongside silently, not wanting their presence known? Companions of the night from among the djinns? Her right hand dropped the rein and checked at her belt for her knife. There it was. Her heart thumped at the thought of enemies in the night—robbers who might think she was carrying something precious, not the message, but gems or a bag of gold. *Thump, thump, thump.* Was it her heart or . . .?

There was someone else in the desert behind her, someone riding at enormous speed in pursuit of her. She knew the thudding was not her heart because her heart seemed to have suddenly stopped. She forced herself to be calm, made her mind melt into the still smoothness of the night. Her senses cleared and she became fully alert.

She slowed down her pace and concentrated, listening with her whole body. There was more than one rider. Yes, two riders. And she had no doubt they were coming after her.

Stillness was her only protection now. If she became motionless, they would not be able to detect her. So horse and rider fused into one. She began to grow cold as the desert air clung and pressed on her clammy skin.

The riders were coming close, very close. She could feel their movements, little rushes of air and swirls of sand brushing against her, as they tried to locate her. She could hear their voices. Ali. She recognized the voice of Ali. And who was that with him?

'She is around us somewhere, Zubayr,' Ali said. He made his horse perform a sort of jump. The impact of his hooves kicked up a flurry of sharp sand. Her horse backed away as some grains shot up his nostrils, prickled his skin.

The next moment, they were flanking her. She grabbed for her knife. But the glint of metal betrayed her. An arm seized her wrist. Ali and Zubayr grappled her off the horse. Her black headdress dashed to the ground. Her hair fell around her shoulders in tangled disarray. The piece of parchment rustled out of its nest. The game was over.

Back in Yathrab, Ali held the piece of parchment up to Hatib, who hung his head. His eyes filled with tears. 'I wanted to save my family. I meant no harm.' He described the sadness he felt at the persecutions and the losses they had suffered after he left. 'I could not bear them to think I had betrayed them.'

The Prophet listened and stroked Hatib's bowed head. 'I understand,' he replied. 'Who am I to hold this against you? But you must realize that the safety of one family must not be bought at the risk of many others. Still, I understand what motivated you. God is merciful. He forgives the man who asks for forgiveness.'

The companions marvelled at Muhammad's compassion as they went about their business. They had a great deal to learn from God's messenger. And there was much to do now as they prepared to set out on the road to Makka.

At six-thirty in the morning of the tenth day of Ramadan, the first stretch of the route from Yathrab to Makka grew dark with tents. Muhammad's army was on the march. The largest army ever to leave the City of Light moved swiftly towards its destination. And along the way, it grew in size. One after another of the Bedouin tribes joined the ranks of the Muslims. Two tribes brought a thousand men each. Steady of purpose, firm of gait, the army surged ahead. True, each man had his own thoughts on how the goal would be achieved, but beneath the banner of God's messenger they were determined to do it right—for it was God himself who directed them.

From one prayer to the next, the day passed swiftly, merging into night. And each day blended into the next, until they came to rest on the seventh night on Marr a'Zahran.

Ten thousand men laid down their weapons. Nearly as many again disengaged the tents and set them up for the night. The men rested, catching breath. The women unstrapped the food and water from the mounts. The animals were fed and watered.

The Prophet stood before them. 'Light a fire, each one of you, at the entrance to your tent. Give the people of Makka notice that we are on our way. Let their leaders see how many we are.'

Imagine the glory! Ten thousand blazing fires reach up to heaven, sending their sparks dancing in a starry stream to join their glittering fellows on high.

Imagine the fear in the heart of Abu Sufyan as he leaps on his horse and creeps to the top of the hill where Muhammad's men wait. He knows he will be safe from the army. These Muslims have their rules of good conduct. Still, he shivers at what could happen. He quails at the destruction that could be inflicted on his possessions and his city. 'Why,' he asks himself for the hundredth time, 'did we not discourage the breaches of the truce?' But it is too late now. He drags himself onwards. Will he have any success this time? Or will his mission fail again like the trip to Makka?

Abu Sufyan starts at the voice in his ear. 'Abu Sufyan? Is this you?'

'It is,' replies Abu Sufyan. 'Who are you?'

'I am Abbas, uncle of the Messenger,' the voice says. 'Have you come to join us?'

'I have come to ask your leader for peace.' There is a pleading note in Abu Sufyan's voice.

'Then ride with me,' Abbas offers. 'I will take you directly to the Prophet.'

'And I will ask him to forgive the people of Makka for breaking the truce. We intend to maintain the truce from now on.'

'It is too late now for that,' the Prophet declared. 'We have to let all the people of Makka know that the promises and lives of men and women are precious. But go back to Makka with this message: all those who take refuge in your home or close the doors of their dwellings will be safe.'

As Abu Sufyan left, the army packed its tents and stood ready for their orders. Muhammad divided the army into four battalions. Zubayr's men were to enter Makka from the north;

Khalid, with his Bedouins, would move in from the southern suburbs; Sa'd ibn Obada would lead the men from Madina into the western quarter; and Abu Obeida would accompany Muhammad in leading the companions around the base of Jebel Hind. The divisions were positioned so that if one group was in trouble, any of the others could easily hasten from the rear to its support.

'But,' said Muhammad, his voice grave and powerful, 'there will be no shedding of blood, no unnecessary violence.'

An ancient man drags himself up a hill overlooking Makka. He is the father of Abu Bakr Siddiq, Muhammad's close companion and father-in-law. Weak, and blind, his hair white as the virgin snow, he toils up, inch by inch, led by his daughter.

'What do you see, my child?' he asks her.

'I see a dark mass, Father. It is billowing out like smoke from the valley, spreading all around.'

'Then take me home,' says the old man. 'Muhammad is coming. I'll meet my son soon.'

The people of Makka listened carefully to the message from Muhammad. Swiftly, they flew to their homes, closing and bolting their doors. But as the streets of the city grew still and silent, one group of men swarmed out and ranged themselves in wait. They were the Bani Bakr. Muhammad's old enemy Umayyah was at their head.

As Khalid's battalion approached, each man crouched on one knee like one massive being. They pulled on the strings of their bows in one united movement and released their arrows together.

Khalid's men saw the volley darken the air like an enraged swarm of locusts. They scattered and ducked, avoiding the attack. The Bedouins behind Khalid roared in protest. There was a wildness in their nature, a fiery determination to protect their honour. They brooked no insult, accepted no overlord. But they obeyed Khalid.

When the Bani Bakr saw no retaliation to their attack, they came forward to fight. Egged on by the roaring Bedouins at his back, Khalid accepted their challenge. He raised his arm, signalling the charge. The next moment, the Bedouins surged forward ready for the test.

Up on the mountain, Muhammad saw the darting lights of sunbeams glinting on the clashing swords.

'Did I not strictly forbid bloodshed?' he demanded enraged.

Someone explained that the Bani Bakr had attacked. Muhammad was somewhat pacified.

The battle seemed to be dying down. Khalid and his men were not fighting needlessly. The Prophet saw the Bani Bakr turn and run, and Khalid and his men pursuing at a distance to the outer limits of Makka. The cowards were escaping to the sea.

By the time the Prophet entered Makka, the city was calm and quiet.

'Would the Prophet like to enter his house?' the people asked.

Muhammad shook his head. He no longer laid claim to any house in Makka—not after so many years away. So, a tent was set up for him. Outside, a cry of 'Allah-o-Akbar' went up. Some soldiers planted the banner of Islam at the opening of the tent.

The Prophet came to the door. The city of Makka was at his feet and, for the most part, its streets had been saved from the stains of blood.

Muhammad left his tent and walked in silence to the Ka'aba. As always, he kissed the stone, offered his prayers and remained in meditation for a long while, thanking God for His blessings. Then he stood up and addressed the people.

'Truth has come,' he said. 'Falsehood has vanished.' He let his eyes wander along the surroundings of the Ka'aba and beyond.

'You are the best and most beloved city to me,' he said, addressing Makka. 'If I had not been forced out of your boundaries, I would never have left you.'

Then he turned to the people of Madina who had given him sanctuary and made him feel so welcome. He saw the concern in their eyes. Now that Muhammad had reclaimed his homeland, would he abandon them and come to live here?

'Where you live,' he promised them, 'there I shall live. And there I will die.'

A cheer went up from the people of Madina.

The Prophet turned to the people of Makka. 'The Lord made Makka a holy and sacred place when He created the universe. I want an end to bloodshed. Let it be known that I personally will compensate anyone who is seeking recompense for murder. Let those who are present tell those who are not.'

And so it was that without turning its soil and pavements red, Muhammad broke the bonds of resentment, anger and greed that had tethered and strapped Makka for so many years. Makka now welcomed back those who had been shunned and driven from it with its holy arms outspread for peace and devotion.

Salek put down the last piece of papyrus. He walked slowly out into the dawn, towards the mosque. He would cleanse himself there and be ready, waiting when the muezzin came to call the sleepers to prayer.

Suddenly he knew why his father had urged him in this direction. If he had failed to provide his son with what he needed, he had ensured he would find it here, among the companions of the Messenger. He had sent Salek on a journey in which he had discovered all that had been lacking in his own life: an entire world of human love and generosity. Silently, he thanked his father.

When Anas took him to meet the Prophet later, he would at last know the purpose of his visit. And he would achieve what perhaps Al-Shair had never achieved. He would accept the message in the presence of the Apostle of God.